This page
Maeve, by Marie Wallin,
pattern page 28

Opposite
Aoife, by Antoni & Alison,
pattern page 48

4

This page
Niamh, *by Marie Wallin,*
pattern page 53

Opposite
Branwen, *pattern page 46*
& Sinead Belt, *pattern page 33*
both by Marie Wallin

This page
Dylan, by Marie Wallin,
pattern page 50

Opposite
Woodland, by Marie Wallin,
pattern page 44

This page
Morrigan, by Marie Wallin,
pattern page 41

Opposite
Ailish Bag, by Marie Wallin,
pattern page 43

Her
Fea, by Marie Wallin,
pattern page 34

Him
Silas, by Marie Wallin,
pattern page 38

13

This page
Elva Scarf, by Marie Wallin,
pattern page 52

Opposite
Heather, by Marie Wallin,
pattern page 26

This page
Keris, by Marie Wallin,
pattern page 24

Opposite
Fea, by Marie Wallin,
pattern page 34

This page
Maple, by Marie Wallin,
pattern page 30

Opposite
Branwen, by Marie Wallin,
pattern page 46

Her
Heather, by Marie Wallin,
pattern page 26

Him
Dylan, by Marie Wallin,
pattern page 50

SIZING GUIDE

Our sizing now conforms to standard clothing sizes. Therefore if you buy a standard size 12 in clothing, then our size 12 or Medium patterns will fit you perfectly.

Dimensions in the charts shown are body measurements, not garment dimensions, therefore please refer to the measuring guide to help you to determine which is the best size for you to knit.

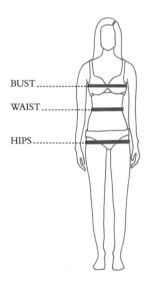

BUST

WAIST

HIPS

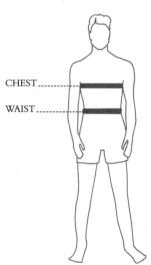

CHEST

WAIST

STANDARD SIZING GUIDE FOR WOMEN

UK SIZE	8	10	12	14	16	18	20	22	
USA Size	6	8	10	12	14	16	18	20	
EUR Size	34	36	38	40	42	44	46	48	
To fit bust	32	34	36	38	40	42	44	46	inches
	82	87	92	97	102	107	112	117	cm
To fit waist	24	26	28	30	32	34	36	38	inches
	61	66	71	76	81	86	91	96	cm
To fit hips	34	36	38	40	42	44	46	48	inches
	87	92	97	102	107	112	117	122	cm

CASUAL SIZING GUIDE FOR WOMEN

As there are some designs that are intended to fit more generously, we have introduced our casual sizing guide. The designs that fall into this group can be recognised by the size range: Small, Medium, Large & Xlarge. Each of these sizes cover two sizes from the standard sizing guide, ie. Size S will fit sizes 8/10, size M will fit sizes 12/14 and so on.

The sizing within this chart is also based on the larger size within the range, ie. M will be based on size 14.

UK SIZE	S	M	L	XL	
DUAL SIZE	8/10	12/14	16/18	20/22	
To fit bust	32 – 34	36 – 38	40 – 42	44 – 46	inches
	82 – 87	92 - 97	102 – 107	112 – 117	cm
To fit waist	24 – 26	28 – 30	32 – 34	36 – 38	inches
	61 – 66	71 – 76	81 – 86	91 – 96	cm
To fit hips	34 – 36	38 – 40	42 – 44	46 – 48	inches
	87 – 92	97 – 102	107 – 112	117 – 122	cm

STANDARD SIZING GUIDE FOR MEN

UK SIZE	S	M	L	XL	XXL	
EUR Size	50	52	54	56	58	
To fit chest	40	42	44	46	48	inches
	102	107	112	117	122	cm
To fit waist	32	34	36	38	40	inches
	81	86	91	96	101	cm

MEASURING GUIDE

For maximum comfort and to ensure the correct fit when choosing a size to knit, please follow the tips below when checking your size.

Measure yourself close to your body, over your underwear and don't pull the tape measure too tight!

Bust/chest – measure around the fullest part of the bust/chest and across the shoulder blades.

Waist – measure around the natural waistline, just above the hip bone.

Hips – measure around the fullest part of the bottom. If you don't wish to measure yourself, note the size of a favourite jumper that you like the fit of. Our sizes are now comparable to the clothing sizes from the major high street retailers, so if your favourite jumper is a size Medium or size 12, then our casual size Medium and standard size 12 should be approximately the same fit.

To be extra sure, measure your favourite jumper and then compare these measurements with the Rowan size diagram given at the end of the individual instructions.

Finally, once you have decided which size is best for you, please ensure that you achieve the tension required for the design you wish to knit.

Remember if your tension is too loose, your garment will be bigger than the pattern size and you may use more yarn. If your tension is too tight, your garment could be smaller than the pattern size and you will have yarn left over.

Furthermore if your tension is incorrect, the handle of your fabric will be too stiff or floppy and will not fit properly. It really does make sense to check your tension before starting every project.

GALLERY

SIZE KEY

■ SIZE 8 - 18   ▲ SIZE S - XL   ★ SIZE S - XXL (MENS)

● SIZE 8 - 22   ◆ SIZE S - L   ✚ ACCESSORY
(Refer to pattern page)

● **WOODLAND**
by MARIE WALLIN
Main image page 3 & 8
Pattern page 44

★ **KERIS**
by MARIE WALLIN
Main image page 3 & 17
Pattern page 24

■ **MAEVE**
by MARIE WALLIN
Main image page 4
Pattern page 28

● **AOIFE**
by ANTONI & ALISON
Main image page 5
Pattern page 48

■ **BRANWEN**
by MARIE WALLIN
Main image page 6 & 19
Pattern page 46

✚ **SINEAD BELT**
by MARIE WALLIN
Main image page 6
Pattern page 33

◆ **NIAMH**
by MARIE WALLIN
Main image page 7
Pattern page 53

★ **DYLAN**
by MARIE WALLIN
Main image page 9 & 21
Pattern page 50

✚ **AILISH BAG**
by MARIE WALLIN
Main image page 10
Pattern page 43

★ **MORRIGAN**
by MARIE WALLIN
Main image page 11
Pattern page 41

▲ **FEA**
by MARIE WALLIN
Main image page 12 & 16
Pattern page 34

★ **SILAS**
by MARIE WALLIN
Main image page 13
Pattern page 38

● **HEATHER**
by MARIE WALLIN
Main image page 14 & 21
Pattern page 26

✚ **ELVA SCARF**
by MARIE WALLIN
Main image page 15
Pattern page 52

■ **MAPLE**
by MARIE WALLIN
Main image page 18
Pattern page 30

Main image page 3 & 17

KERIS

by MARIE WALLIN

SIZE

	S	M	L	XL	XXL	
To fit chest						
	102	107	112	117	122	cm
	40	42	44	46	48	in

YARN

Rowan Country and Big Wool

A	Country Ash 651					
	12	13	14	15	15	x 50gm
B	Big Wool Sandstone 040					
	1	1	1	1	1	x 100gm
C	Big Wool Forest 043					
	1	1	1	1	1	x 100gm
D	Big Wool Acer 041					
	1	1	1	1	1	x 100gm

NEEDLES

1 pair 8mm (no 0) (US 11) needles
1 pair 9mm (no 00) (US 13) needles

TENSION

10 sts and 14 rows to 10 cm measured over stocking stitch using 9mm (US 13) needles.

BACK

Using 8mm (US 11) needles and yarn A cast on 58 [60: 64: 66: 70] sts.
Row 1 (RS): K0 [1: 0: 0: 0], P2 [2: 1: 2: 0], *K2, P2, rep from * to last 0 [1: 3: 0: 2] sts, K0 [1: 2: 0: 2], P0 [0: 1: 0: 0].
Row 2: P0 [1: 0: 0: 0], K2 [2: 1: 2: 0], *P2, K2, rep from * to last 0 [1: 3: 0: 2] sts, P0 [1: 2: 0: 2], K0 [0: 1: 0: 0].
These 2 rows form rib.
Work in rib for a further 6 rows, ending with RS facing for next row.
Change to 9mm (US 13) needles.
Beg with a P row, work in rev st st until back meas 18 [19: 18: 19: 18] cm, ending with RS facing for next row.
Next row (RS): P28 [29: 31: 32: 34], K2, P to end.
Next row: K28 [29: 31: 32: 34], P2, K to end.
These 2 rows set the sts.
Cont as set for a further 9 rows, ending with **WS** facing for next row.
Next row (WS): K20 [21: 23: 24: 26], P2, K6, P2, K to end.
Next row: P28 [29: 31: 32: 34], K2, P6, K2, P to end.
These 2 rows set the sts.
Cont as set for a further 11 rows, ending with RS

facing for next row.
Next row (RS): P20 [21: 23: 24: 26], (K2, P6) twice, K2, P to end.
Next row: K20 [21: 23: 24: 26], (P2, K6) twice, P2, K to end.
These 2 rows set the sts.
Cont as set until back meas 39 [40: 39: 40: 39] cm, ending with RS facing for next row.
Shape armholes
Keeping patt correct, cast off 2 sts at beg of next 2 rows.
54 [56: 60: 62: 66] sts.
Next row (RS): P2tog, P16 [17: 19: 20: 22], (K2, P6) 3 times, K2, P to last 2 sts, P2tog.
Next row: K2tog, K7 [8: 10: 11: 13], (P2, K6) 3 times, P2, K to last 2 sts, K2tog.
50 [52: 56: 58: 62] sts.
These 2 rows set the sts.
Cont as set, dec 1 st at each end of next 2 [1: 1: 0: 0] rows.
46 [50: 54: 58: 62] sts.
Work a further 4 [5: 5: 6: 6] rows, ending with RS facing for next row
Next row (RS): P6 [8: 10: 12: 14], (K2, P6) 4 times, K2, P to end.
Next row: K6 [8: 10: 12: 14], (P2, K6) 4 times, P2, K to end.
These 2 rows set the sts.
Cont straight until armhole meas 22 [23: 24: 25: 26] cm, ending with RS facing for next row.
Shape shoulders and back neck
Next row (RS): Cast off 6 [7: 8: 9: 10] sts, patt until there are 10 [11: 11: 12: 13] sts on right needle and turn, leaving rem sts on a holder.
Work each side of neck separately.
Cast off 3 sts at beg of next row.
Cast off rem 7 [8: 8: 9: 10] sts.
With RS facing, rejoin yarn to rem sts, cast off centre 14 [14: 16: 16: 16] sts, patt to end.
Complete to match first side, reversing shapings.

FRONT

Work as given for back until 6 [6: 8: 8: 10] rows less have been worked than on back to beg of shoulder shaping, ending with RS facing for next row.
Shape neck
Next row (RS): Patt 16 [18: 20: 22: 24] sts and turn, leaving rem sts on a holder.
Work each side of neck separately.
Dec 1 st at neck edge of next 2 rows, then on foll 1 [1: 2: 2: 2] alt rows.

13 [15: 16: 18: 20] sts.
Work 1 row, ending with RS facing for next row.
Shape shoulder
Cast off 6 [7: 8: 9: 10] sts at beg of next row.
Work 1 row.
Cast off rem 7 [8: 8: 9: 10] sts.
With RS facing, rejoin yarn to rem sts, cast off centre 14 sts, patt to end.
Complete to match first side, reversing shapings.

SLEEVES
Using 8mm (US 11) needles cast on 26 [28: 28: 30: 30] sts.
Row 1 (RS): K0 [1: 1: 2: 2], P2, ★K2, P2, rep from ★ to last 0 [1: 1: 2: 2] sts, K0 [1: 1: 2: 2].
Row 2: P0 [1: 1: 2: 2], K2, ★P2, K2, rep from ★ to last 0 [1: 1: 2: 2] sts, P0 [1: 1: 2: 2].
These 2 rows form rib.
Work in rib for a further 6 rows, ending with RS facing for next row.
Change to 9mm (US 13) needles.
Beg with a P row, work in rev st st, shaping sides by inc 1 st at each end of 5th and every foll 4th row to 36 [34: 38: 36: 40] sts, then on every foll 6th row until there are 40 [42: 44: 46: 48] sts.
Work 4 rows, ending with **WS** facing for next row.
Next row (WS): K19 [20: 21: 22: 23], P2, K to end.
Next row: Inc in first st, P18 [19: 20: 21: 22], K2, P to last st, inc in last st.
42 [44: 46: 48: 50: 52] sts.
These 2 rows set the sts.
Cont as set for a further 9 rows, inc 1 st at each end of 6th of these rows and ending with RS facing for next row.
44 [46: 48: 50: 52] sts.
Next row (RS): P21 [22: 23: 24: 25], K2, P6, K2, P to end.
Next row: K13 [14: 15: 16: 17], P2, K6, P2, K to end.
These 2 rows set the sts.
Cont as set for a further 5 rows, inc 1 st at each end of first of these rows and ending with **WS**

facing for next row.
46 [48: 50: 52: 54] sts.
Next row (WS): K14 [15: 16: 17: 18], (P2, K6) twice, P2, K to end.
Next row: Inc in first st, P13 [14: 15: 16: 17], (K2, P6) 3 times, K2, P to last st, inc in last st.
48 [50: 52: 54: 56] sts.
Next row: K7 [8: 9: 10: 11], (P2, K6) 3 times, P2, K to end.
Last 2 rows set the sts.
Cont as set for a further 3 rows, ending with **WS** facing for next row.
Next row (WS): K7 [8: 9: 10: 11], (P2, K6) 4 times, P2, K to end.
Next row: P7 [8: 9: 10: 11], (K2, P6) 4 times, K2, P to end.
These 2 rows set the sts for rest of sleeve.
Work 1 row, ending with RS facing for next row.
(Sleeve should meas 52 [54: 56: 58: 60] cm.)
Shape top
Keeping patt correct, cast off 2 sts at beg of next 2 rows.
44 [46: 48: 50: 52] sts.
Dec 1 st at each end of next 5 rows, then on every foll alt row to 32 sts, then on foll 7 rows, ending with RS facing for next row. 18 sts.
Cast off 5 sts at beg of next 2 rows.
Cast off rem 8 sts.

MAKING UP
Press as described on the information page.
Join right shoulder seam using back stitch, or mattress stitch if preferred.
Collar
With RS facing, using 8mm (US 11) needles and yarn A, pick up and knit 7 [7: 9: 9: 11] sts down left side of neck, 14 sts from front, 7 [7: 9: 9: 11] sts up right side of neck, then 18 [18: 22: 22: 22] sts from back.
46 [46: 54: 54: 58] sts.
Row 1 (WS): K2, ★P2, K2, rep from ★ to end.
Row 2: P2, ★K2, P2, rep from ★ to end.
These 2 rows form rib.
Work in rib until collar meas 16 cm, ending with

RS facing for next row.
Cast off in rib.
See information page for finishing instructions, setting in sleeves using the set-in method.
Using photograph as a guide and yarns B, C and D, oversew along each pair of K sts on front, back and sleeves.

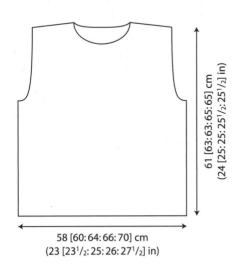

61 [63: 63: 65: 65] cm
(24 [25: 25: 25½: 25½] in)

58 [60: 64: 66: 70] cm
(23 [23½: 25: 26: 27½] in)

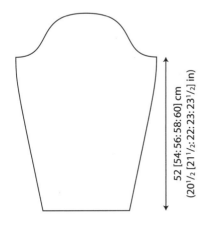

52 [54: 56: 58: 60] cm
(20½ [21½: 22: 23: 23½] in)

Main image page 14 & 21

HEATHER

by MARIE WALLIN

SIZE

8	10	12	14	16	18	20	22	

To fit bust

82	87	92	97	102	107	112	117	cm
32	34	36	38	40	42	44	46	in

YARN
Rowan Country
A Birch 650

4	4	5	5	5	6	6	6	x 50gm

B Damson 658

6	6	6	7	7	7	8	8	x 50gm

C Reed 659

1	1	1	2	2	2	2	2	x 50gm

D Juniper 654

1	1	2	2	2	2	2	2	x 50gm

NEEDLES

1 pair 9mm (no 00) (US 13) needles
8.00mm (no 0) (US L11) crochet hook

BUTTONS – 5 x 00410

TENSION

10 sts and 19 rows to 10 cm measured over garter stitch using 9mm (US 13) needles.

UK CROCHET ABBREVIATIONS

ch = chain; **ss** = slip stitch; **dc** = double crochet;
tr = treble; **sp** = space.

US CROCHET ABBREVIATIONS

ch = chain; **ss** = slip stitch; **dc** = single crochet;
tr = double; **sp** = space.

BACK
Using 9mm (US 13) needles and yarn A cast on
45 [47: 49: 53: 55: 59: 61: 65] sts.
Row 1 (WS): Knit.
Joining in colours as required, work in striped g st
as folls:
Rows 2 and 3: Using yarn B, knit.
Rows 4 and 5: Using yarn C, knit.
Rows 6 and 7: Using yarn D, knit.
Rows 8 and 9: Using yarn A, knit.
Rows 2 to 9 form striped g st.
Cont in striped g st, shaping side seams by
dec 1 st at each end of 5th and every foll 6th row
until 39 [41: 43: 47: 49: 53: 55: 59] sts rem.
Work 9 rows, ending with RS facing for next row.
Inc 1 st at each end of next and foll 10th row.
43 [45: 47: 51: 53: 57: 59: 63] sts.
Cont straight until back meas 34 [34: 33: 36:

35: 37: 36: 38] cm, ending with RS facing for
next row.
Shape armholes
Keeping stripes correct, cast off 3 sts at beg of
next 2 rows. 37 [39: 41: 45: 47: 51: 53: 57] sts.
Dec 1 st at each end of next 1 [1: 1: 3: 3: 3: 3: 5]
rows, then on foll 1 [1: 2: 1: 1: 3: 3: 2] alt rows.
33 [35: 35: 37: 39: 39: 41: 43] sts.
Cont straight until armhole meas 21 [21: 22: 22:
23: 23: 24: 24] cm, ending with RS facing for
next row.
Shape shoulders and back neck
Next row (RS): Cast off 2 [3: 3: 3: 3: 3: 4: 4] sts,
K until there are 6 [6: 6: 7: 7: 7: 7: 8] sts on right
needle and turn, leaving rem sts on a holder.
Work each side of neck separately.
Cast off 3 sts at beg of next row.
Cast off rem 3 [3: 3: 4: 4: 4: 4: 5] sts.
With RS facing, rejoin appropriate yarn to rem
sts, cast off centre 17 [17: 17: 17: 19: 19: 19: 19] sts,
K to end.
Complete to match first side, reversing shapings.

LEFT FRONT
Using 9mm (US 13) needles and yarn A cast on
21 [22: 23: 25: 26: 28: 29: 31] sts.
Row 1 (WS): Knit.
Joining in colours as required, work in striped g st
as given for back, shaping side seam by dec 1 st at
beg of 13th and every foll 6th row until 18 [19:
20: 22: 23: 25: 26: 28] sts rem.
Work 9 rows, ending with RS facing for next row.
Inc 1 st at beg of next and foll 10th row.
20 [21: 22: 24: 25: 27: 28: 30] sts.
Cont straight until left front matches back to beg
of armhole shaping, ending with RS facing for
next row.
Shape armhole
Keeping stripes correct, cast off 3 sts at beg
of next row.
17 [18: 19: 21: 22: 24: 25: 27] sts.
Work 1 row.
Dec 1 st at armhole edge of next 1 [1: 1: 3: 3:
3: 3: 5] rows, then on foll 1 [1: 2: 1: 1: 3: 3: 2]
alt rows.
15 [16: 16: 17: 18: 18: 19: 20] sts.
Cont straight until 9 [9: 9: 11: 11: 11: 13: 13] rows
less have been worked than on back to beg of
shoulder shaping, ending with **WS** facing for
next row.
Shape neck
Keeping stripes correct, cast off 6 [6: 6: 5: 6: 6:

5: 5] sts at beg of next row.
9 [10: 10: 12: 12: 12: 14: 15] sts.
Dec 1 st at neck edge of next 3 rows, then on foll 1 [1: 1: 2: 2: 2: 3: 3] alt rows.
5 [6: 6: 7: 7: 7: 8: 9] sts.
Work 3 rows, ending with RS facing for next row.

Shape shoulder
Cast off 2 [3: 3: 3: 3: 3: 4: 4] sts at beg of next row.
Work 1 row.
Cast off rem 3 [3: 3: 4: 4: 4: 4: 5] sts.

RIGHT FRONT
Using 9mm (US 13) needles and yarn A cast on 21 [22: 23: 25: 26: 28: 29: 31] sts.
Row 1 (WS): Knit.
Joining in colours as required, work in striped g st as given for back, shaping side seam by dec 1 st at end of 13th and every foll 6th row until 18 [19: 20: 22: 23: 25: 26: 28] sts rem.
Complete to match left front, reversing shapings.

SLEEVES
Using 9mm (US 13) needles and yarn A cast on 26 [26: 28: 28: 30: 30: 32: 32] sts.
Row 1 (WS): Knit.
Joining in colours as required, work in striped g st as given for back, shaping sides by inc 1 st at each end of 9th and every foll 10th row to 38 [38: 38: 38: 38: 38: 42: 42] sts, then on every foll 12th row until there are 40 [40: 42: 42: 44: 44: 46: 46] sts.
Cont straight until sleeve meas 43 [43: 44: 44: 45: 45: 44: 44] cm, ending with RS facing for next row.

Shape top
Keeping stripes correct, cast off 3 sts at beg of next 2 rows. 34 [34: 36: 36: 38: 38: 40: 40] sts.
Dec 1 st at each end of next 3 rows, then on every foll alt row to 8 sts, then on foll row, ending with RS facing for next row.
Cast off rem 6 sts.

MAKING UP
Press as described on the information page.
Join both shoulder seams using back stitch, or mattress stitch if preferred.
See information page for finishing instructions, setting in sleeves using the set-in method.
Mark positions for 5 buttonholes along right front opening edge – lowest buttonhole 5 cm up from cast-on edge, top buttonhole just below neck shaping, and rem 3 buttonholes evenly spaced between.

Edging
With **WS** facing, using 8.00mm (US L11) crochet hook and yarn B, attach yarn at base of one side seam, 1 ch (does NOT count as st), work 1 round of dc evenly around entire hem, front opening and neck edges, working 3 dc into corner dc and ending with ss to first dc.
Next round (WS): 1 ch (does NOT count as st), 1 dc into each dc to end, missing dc as required around neck edge to ensure edging lays flat and that number of dc (between corner dc) is divisible by 3, working 3 dc into corners, making buttonholes at positions marked by replacing (1 dc into next dc) with (1 ch, miss 1 dc) and ending with ss to first dc.
Fasten off.
Mark 2nd dc in from each corner point – number of dc between markers should be divisible by 3 plus 2.

Right front edging
With **WS** facing, using 8.00mm (US L11) crochet hook and yarn B, attach yarn at top of right front opening edge, 1 ch (does NOT count as st), work down right front opening edge as folls: 1 dc into each dc and ch sp to lower edge.
Fasten off.

Left front edging
With **WS** facing, using 8.00mm (US L11) crochet hook and yarn B, attach yarn at base of left front opening edge, 1 ch (does NOT count as st), work up left front opening edge as folls: 1 dc into each dc to neck edge.
Fasten off.

Collar
With RS facing, using 8.00mm (US L11) crochet hook and yarn B, attach yarn to marked dc at right neck edge, 5 ch (counts as 1 tr and 2 ch), miss dc where yarn was attached and next 2 dc, *3 tr into next dc, 2 ch, miss 2 dc, rep from * to marked dc at left neck edge, 1 tr into this marked dc, turn.
Next row: 3 ch (counts as first tr), 2 tr into first ch sp, *2 ch, miss 3 tr, 3 tr into next ch sp, rep from * to end, working tr at end of last rep into 3rd of 5 ch at beg of previous row, turn.
Next row: 5 ch (counts as 1 tr and 2 ch), miss 3 tr at end of previous row, *3 tr into next ch sp, 2 ch, miss 3 tr, rep from * to last 3 sts, 2 ch, miss 2 tr, 1 tr into top of 3 ch at beg of previous row, turn.
Rep last 2 rows once more.
Fasten off.

Cuff edging
With RS facing, using 8.00mm (US L11) crochet hook and yarn B, attach yarn at base of one sleeve seam, 1 ch (does NOT count as st), work 1 round of dc evenly around cast-on edge of sleeve, ending with ss to first dc.
Next round (RS): 1 ch (does NOT count as st), 1 dc into each dc to end, ss to first dc.
Fasten off.

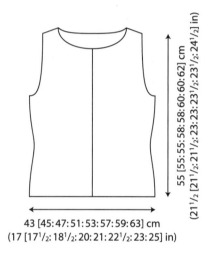

55 [55: 55: 58: 58: 60: 60: 62] cm
(21½ [21½: 21½: 23: 23: 23½: 23½: 24½] in)

43 [45: 47: 51: 53: 57: 59: 63] cm
(17 [17½: 18½: 20: 21: 22½: 23: 25] in)

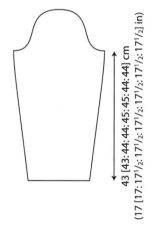

43 [43: 44: 44: 45: 45: 44: 44] cm
(17 [17: 17½: 17½: 17½: 17½: 17½: 17½] in)

Main image page 4

■ ■

MAEVE

by MARIE WALLIN

SIZE

8	10	12	14	16	18	
To fit bust						
82	87	92	97	102	107	cm
32	34	36	38	40	42	in

YARN

Rowan Country

14	14	15	16	17	18	x 50gm

(photographed in Damson 658)

NEEDLES

1 pair 9mm (no 00) (US 13) needles
8.00mm (no 0) (US L11) crochet hook

BUTTONS - 1 x 00356

TENSION

10 sts and 14 rows to 10 cm measured over stocking stitch using 9mm (US 13) needles.

UK CROCHET ABBREVIATIONS

ch = chain; **dc** = double crochet; **sp** = space;
tr = treble.

US CROCHET ABBREVIATIONS

ch = chain; **dc** = single crochet; **sp** = space;
tr = double.

BACK

Using 9mm (US 13) needles cast on 44 [46: 48: 52: 54: 58] sts.
Beg with a K row, work in st st, shaping side seams by dec 1 st at each end of 9th and foll 6th row.
40 [42: 44: 48: 50: 54] sts.
Work 9 rows, ending with RS facing for next row.
Inc 1 st at each end of next and foll 10th row.
44 [46: 48: 52: 54: 58] sts.
Cont straight until back meas 34 [34: 33: 36: 35: 37] cm, ending with RS facing for next row.
Shape armholes
Cast off 3 sts at beg of next 2 rows.
38 [40: 42: 46: 48: 52] sts.
Dec 1 st at each end of next 2 [3: 3: 4: 5: 6] rows.
34 [34: 36: 38: 38: 40] sts.
Cont straight until armhole meas 20 [20: 21: 21: 22: 22] cm, ending with RS facing for next row.
Shape shoulders and back neck
Next row (RS): Cast off 4 [4: 5: 5: 5: 5] sts, K until there are 8 [8: 8: 9: 8: 9] sts on right needle and turn, leaving rem sts on a holder.
Work each side of neck separately.

Cast off 3 sts at beg of next row.
Cast off rem 5 [5: 5: 6: 5: 6] sts.
With RS facing, rejoin yarn to rem sts, cast off centre 10 [10: 10: 10: 12: 12] sts, K to end.
Complete to match first side, reversing shapings.

LEFT FRONT

Using 9mm (US 13) needles cast on 21 [22: 23: 25: 26: 28] sts.
Beg with a K row, work in st st, shaping side seam by dec 1 st at beg of 9th and foll 6th row.
19 [20: 21: 23: 24: 26] sts.
Work 9 rows, ending with RS facing for next row.
Inc 1 st at beg of next and foll 10th row.
21 [22: 23: 25: 26: 28] sts.
Cont straight until left front matches back to beg of armhole shaping, ending with RS facing for next row.
Shape armhole and front slope
Cast off 3 sts at beg and dec 1 st at end of next row.
17 [18: 19: 21: 22: 24] sts.
Work 1 row.
Dec 1 st at armhole edge of next 2 [3: 3: 4: 5: 6] rows **and at same time** dec 1 st at front slope edge of next [next: 3rd: 3rd: next: next] and foll 0 [0: 0: 0: alt: alt] row.
14 [14: 15: 16: 15: 16] sts.
Dec 1 st at front slope edge **only** of 3rd [2nd: 4th: 3rd: 2nd: next] and every foll 4th row until 9 [9: 10: 11: 10: 11] sts rem.
Cont straight until left front matches back to beg of shoulder shaping, ending with RS facing for next row.
Shape shoulder
Cast off 4 [4: 5: 5: 5: 5] sts at beg of next row.
Work 1 row.
Cast off rem 5 [5: 5: 6: 5: 6] sts.

RIGHT FRONT

Using 9mm (US 13) needles cast on 21 [22: 23: 25: 26: 28] sts.
Beg with a K row, work in st st, shaping side seam by dec 1 st at end of 9th and foll 6th row.
19 [20: 21: 23: 24: 26] sts.
Complete to match left front, reversing shapings.

SLEEVES

Using 9mm (US 13) needles cast on 24 [24: 26: 26: 28: 28] sts.
Beg with a K row, work in st st, shaping sides by inc 1 st at each end of 3rd [3rd: 5th: 5th: 5th: 5th]

and every foll 6th row to 38 [38: 40: 40: 40: 40] sts, then on every foll – [–: –: –: 8th: 8th] row until there are – [–: –: –: 42: 42] sts.
Cont straight until sleeve meas 34 [34: 35: 35: 36: 36] cm, ending with RS facing for next row.

Shape top
Cast off 3 sts at beg of next 2 rows.
32 [32: 34: 34: 36: 36] sts.
Dec 1 st at each end of next and foll alt row, then on every foll 4th row until 24 [24: 26: 26: 28: 28] sts rem.
Work 1 row, ending with RS facing for next row.
Dec 1 st at each end of next and every foll alt row to 20 sts, then on foll 3 rows, ending with RS facing for next row.
Cast off rem 14 sts.

MAKING UP
Press as described on the information page.
Join both shoulder seams using back stitch, or mattress stitch if preferred. Join side seams.

Hem edging
With RS facing and using 8.00mm (US L11) crochet hook, attach yarn at base of left front opening edge, 1 ch (does NOT count as st), working evenly across cast-on edges work: 1 dc into first st, ★1 ch, miss 1 st, (1 dc, 3 ch and 1 dc) into next st, 1 dc into next st; rep from ★ to last 2 sts (missing an extra st as required so that 2 sts are left at end of row), 1 ch, 1 dc into last st, turn.
Row 1 (WS): 3 ch (counts as first tr), miss first dc, ★(1 tr, 3 ch, 1 dc into back loop only of last tr worked and 1 tr) into next ch sp★★, 2 ch, miss (2 dc, 3 ch and 1 dc), rep from ★ to end, ending last rep at ★★, 1 tr into last dc, turn.
Row 2: 5 ch (counts as first tr and 2 ch), ★(1 tr, 3 ch, 1 dc into back loop only of last tr worked and 1 tr) into next ch sp, 2 ch, rep from ★ to end, 1 tr into top of 3 ch at beg of previous row, turn.
Row 3: 3 ch (counts as first tr), miss tr at base of 3 ch, ★(1 tr, 3 ch, 1 dc into back loop only of last tr worked and 1 tr) into next ch sp★★, 2 ch, rep from ★ to end, ending last rep at ★★, 1 tr into 3rd of 5 ch at beg of previous row, turn.
Row 4: As row 2.
Fasten off.

Front and neck edging
Work as for hem edging along entire front opening and neck edges, beg and ending at top ends of last row of hem edging and placing sts of base row evenly along row-end edges.

Cuff edging
Work along cast-on edges of sleeves as given for hem edging.
See information page for finishing instructions, setting in sleeves using the set-in method.
Attach button and make button loop to correspond, positioning both on inside of base row of front and neck edging level with beg of front slope shaping.

44 [46: 48: 52: 54: 58] cm
(17½ [18: 19: 20½: 21½: 23] in)

54 [54: 54: 57: 57: 59] cm
(21½ [21½: 21½: 22½: 22½: 23] in)
excluding trim

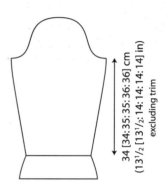

34 [34: 35: 35: 36: 36] cm
(13½ [13½: 14: 14: 14: 14] in)
excluding trim

Main image page 18

MAPLE

by MARIE WALLIN

SIZE

8	10	12	14	16	18	
To fit bust						
82	87	92	97	102	107	cm
32	34	36	38	40	42	in

YARN

Rowan Country

12	12	13	13	14	15	x 50gm

(photographed in Cedarwood 653)

NEEDLES

1 pair 8mm (no 0) (US 11) needles
1 pair 9mm (no 00) (US 13) needles
8mm (no 0) (US 11) circular needle
Cable needle

BEADS – approx 280 [280: 280: 290: 290: 300]
wooden beads ★Ref wooden bead WB5 col. 2
Brown from Creative Bead Craft Ltd.

TENSION

10 sts and 14 rows to 10 cm measured over
stocking stitch using 9mm (US 13) needles.

SPECIAL ABBREVIATIONS

Cr3R = slip next st onto cable needle and leave
at back of work, K2, then P1 from cable needle;
Cr3L = slip next 2 sts onto cable needle and leave
at front of work, P1, then K2 from cable needle;
C4B = slip next 2 sts onto cable needle and leave
at back of work, K2, then K2 from cable needle;
C4F = slip next 2 sts onto cable needle and leave
at front of work, K2, then K2 from cable needle;
C5B = slip next 3 sts onto cable needle and leave
at back of work, K2, slip last st on cable needle
back onto left needle and P this st, then K2 from
cable needle.

BACK

Using 8mm (US 11) needles cast on 47 [49: 51:
55: 57: 61] sts.
Row 1 (RS): K1 [2: 0: 0: 0: 2], P3 [3: 0: 2: 3: 3],
★K3, P3, rep from ★ to last 1 [2: 3: 5: 0: 2] sts,
K1 [2: 3: 3: 0: 2], P0 [0: 0: 2: 0: 0].
Row 2: P1 [2: 0: 0: 0: 2], K3 [3: 0: 2: 3: 3], ★P3,
K3, rep from ★ to last 1 [2: 3: 5: 0: 2] sts, P1 [2: 3:
3: 0: 2], K0 [0: 0: 2: 0: 0].
These 2 rows form rib.
Work in rib for a further 8 rows, ending with RS
facing for next row.
Row 11 (RS): Rib 10 [11: 12: 14: 15: 17],
M1, rib 2, M1, rib 11, M1, rib 1, M1, rib 11,

M1, rib 2, M1, rib to end.
53 [55: 57: 61: 63: 67] sts.
Change to 9mm (US 13) needles.
Beg and ending rows as indicated, repeating the
28 row patt repeat throughout and noting that
chart row 1 is a **WS** row, cont in patt from chart
for back and front as folls:
Work 3 rows, ending with RS facing for next row.
Dec 1 st at each end of next and foll 4th row.
49 [51: 53: 57: 59: 63] sts.
Work 9 rows, ending with RS facing for next row.
Inc 1 st at each end of next and foll 10th row.
53 [55: 57: 61: 63: 67] sts.
Cont straight until back meas 34 [34: 33: 36:
35: 37] cm, ending with RS facing for next row.
Shape armholes
Keeping patt correct, cast off 3 sts at beg of next
2 rows.
47 [49: 51: 55: 57: 61] sts.
Dec 1 st at each end of next 2 [3: 3: 5: 5: 6] rows.
43 [43: 45: 45: 47: 49] sts.
Cont straight until armhole meas 21 [21: 22: 22:
23: 23] cm, ending with RS facing for next row.
Shape shoulders and back neck
Next row (RS): Cast off 5 [5: 6: 6: 6: 6] sts, patt
until there are 10 [10: 10: 10: 10: 11] sts on right
needle and turn, leaving rem sts on a holder.
Work each side of neck separately.
Cast off 4 sts at beg of next row.
Cast off rem 6 [6: 6: 6: 6: 7] sts.
With RS facing, rejoin yarn to rem sts, cast off
centre 13 [13: 13: 13: 15: 15] sts, patt to end.
Complete to match first side, reversing shapings.

FRONT

Work as given for back until 10 rows less have
been worked than on back to beg of shoulder
shaping, ending with RS facing for next row.
Shape neck
Next row (RS): Patt 16 [16: 17: 17: 17: 18] sts
and turn, leaving rem sts on a holder.
Work each side of neck separately.
Dec 1 st at neck edge of next 4 rows, then on
foll alt row.
11 [11: 12: 12: 12: 13] sts.
Work 3 rows, ending with RS facing for next row.
Shape shoulder
Cast off 5 [5: 6: 6: 6: 6] sts at beg of next row.
Work 1 row.
Cast off rem 6 [6: 6: 6: 6: 7] sts.
With RS facing, rejoin yarn to rem sts, cast off
centre 11 [11: 11: 11: 13: 13] sts, patt to end.

Back & front chart

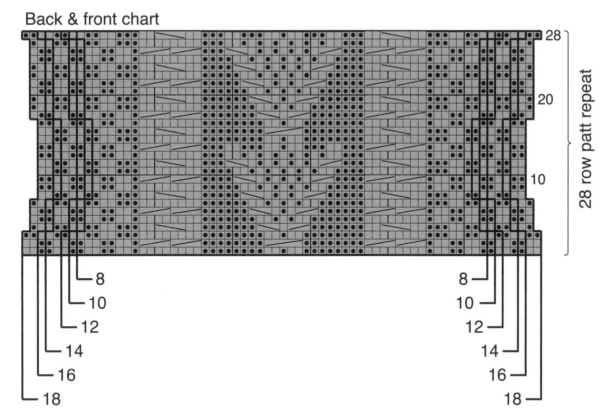

28

20

10

28 row patt repeat

8
10
12
14
16
18

8
10
12
14
16
18

Sleeve chart

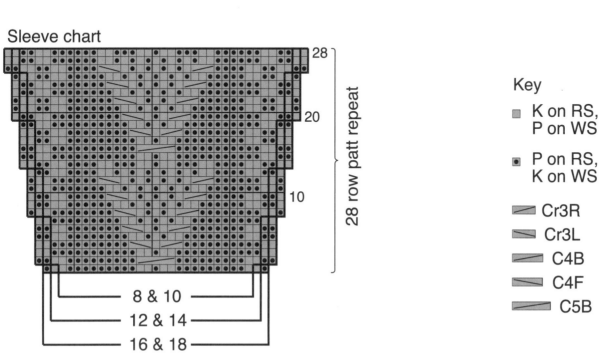

28

20

10

28 row patt repeat

8 & 10
12 & 14
16 & 18

Key

K on RS,
P on WS

P on RS,
K on WS

Cr3R

Cr3L

C4B

C4F

C5B

Complete to match first side, reversing shapings.
SLEEVES
Using 8mm (US 11) needles cast on 23 [23: 25: 25: 27: 27] sts.
Row 1 (RS): K1 [1: 2: 2: 3: 3], P3, *K3, P3, rep from * to last 1 [1: 2: 2: 3: 3] sts, K1 [1: 2: 2: 3: 3].
Row 2: P1 [1: 2: 2: 3: 3], K3, *P3, K3, rep from * to last 1 [1: 2: 2: 3: 3] sts, P1 [1: 2: 2: 3: 3].
These 2 rows form rib.
Work in rib for a further 8 rows, ending with RS facing for next row.
Row 11 (RS): Rib 11 [11: 12: 12: 13: 13], M1, rib 1, M1, rib to end.
25 [25: 27: 27: 29: 29] sts.
Change to 9mm (US 13) needles.
Beg and ending rows as indicated, repeating the 28 row patt repeat throughout and noting that chart row 1 is a **WS** row, cont in patt from chart for sleeves, shaping sides by inc 1 st at each end of 2nd and every foll 6th row to 41 sts, then on every foll – [-: 8th: 8th: 8th: 8th] row until there are – [-: 43: 43: 45: 45] sts, taking inc sts into patt.
Cont straight until sleeve meas 44 [44: 45: 45: 46: 46] cm, ending with RS facing for next row.
Shape top
Keeping patt correct, cast off 3 sts at beg of next 2 rows.
35 [35: 37: 37: 39: 39] sts.
Dec 1 st at each end of next and foll alt row, then on foll 4th row, then on every foll alt row to 23 sts, then on foll 3 rows, ending with RS facing

for next row.
Cast off rem 17 sts.

MAKING UP
Press as described on the information page.
Join both shoulder seams using back stitch, or mattress stitch if preferred.
Neckband
With RS facing and using 8mm (US 11) circular needle, pick up and knit 11 [11: 11: 11: 12: 12] sts down left side of neck, 11 [11: 11: 11: 13: 13] sts

from front, 11 [11: 11: 11: 12: 12] sts up right side of neck, then 21 [21: 21: 21: 23: 23] sts from back.
54 [54: 54: 54: 60: 60] sts.
Round 1 (RS): *K3, P3, rep from * to end.
Rep this round until neckband meas 10 cm.
Cast off in rib.
See information page for finishing instructions, setting in sleeves using the set-in method.
Using photograph as a guide, attach beads to either side of centre V cable panels, and along V cable panels of body and sleeves.

43 [45: 47: 51: 53: 57] cm
(17 [17½: 18½: 20: 21: 22½] in)

55 [55: 55: 58: 58: 60] cm
(21½ [21½: 21½: 23: 23: 23½] in)

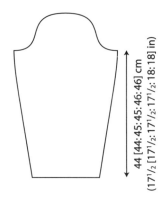

44 [44: 45: 45: 46: 46] cm
(17½ [17½: 17½: 17½: 18: 18] in)

Main image page 6

SINEAD BELT

by MARIE WALLIN

YARN
Rowan Country and Big Wool
A Country Cedarwood 653
        3   x 50gm
B Big Wool Sandstone 040
        1   x 100gm
C Big Wool Forest 043
        1   x 100gm
D Big Wool Acer 041
        1   x 100gm

CROCHET HOOK
8.00mm (no 0) (US L11) crochet hook

EXTRAS – 114 cm of 5 cm wide petersham ribbon, 10 cm x 120 cm piece of lining fabric, 5 cm buckle x 00367 and matching sewing thread

TENSION
12 sts and 5½ rows to 10 cm measured over treble fabric using 8.00mm (US L11) crochet hook.

UK CROCHET ABBREVIATIONS
ch = chain; dc = double crochet; tr = treble.

US CROCHET ABBREVIATIONS
ch = chain; dc = single crochet; tr = double.

FINISHED SIZE
Completed belt measures 5 cm (2 in) wide

and 114 cm (45 in) long.

BELT
Using 8.00mm (US L11) crochet hook and yarn A make 7 ch.
Row 1 (RS): 1 dc into 2nd ch from hook, 1 dc into each of next 5 ch, turn.
6 sts.
Row 2: 3 ch (counts as first tr), miss dc at base of 3 ch, 1 tr into each dc to end, turn.
Row 3: 3 ch (counts as first tr), miss tr at base of 3 ch, 1 tr into each tr to end, working last tr into top of 3 ch at beg of previous row, turn.
Rep row 3 until belt meas 114 cm.
Fasten off.

MAKING UP
Press as described on the information page.
Using photograph as a guide, weave yarns B, C and D in and out of trebles of each row, using yarn DOUBLE.
Lay petersham ribbon onto WS of belt. Trim lining fabric to same size as crochet section, adding seam allowance along all edges. Fold seam allowance to WS, lay lining against crochet section, WS facing, and slip stitch pieces together along all edges.

Attach buckle to one end of belt.

Main image page 12 & 16

░░░

FEA

by MARIE WALLIN

SIZE

	S	M	L	XL	
To fit bust					
	82-87	92-97	102-107	112-117	cm
	32-34	36-38	40-42	44-46	in

YARN

Rowan Country and Big Wool

A	Country Cedarwood 653				
	15	17	19	20	x 50gm
B	Big Wool Acer 041				
	1	1	1	1	x 100gm

NEEDLES

1 pair 9mm (no 00) (US 13) needles
8.00mm (no 0) (US L11) crochet hook
Cable needle

BUTTONS – 5 x 00411

TENSION

10 sts and 14 rows to 10 cm measured over stocking stitch using 9mm (US 13) needles.

SPECIAL ABBREVIATIONS

Cr3R = slip next st onto cable needle and leave at back of work, K2, then P1 from cable needle; **Cr3L** = slip next 2 sts onto cable needle and leave at front of work, P1, then K2 from cable needle; **C4B** = slip next 2 sts onto cable needle and leave at back of work, K2, then K2 from cable needle; **C4F** = slip next 2 sts onto cable needle and leave at front of work, K2, then K2 from cable needle; **loop 6 tog** = with yarn at back (WS) of work insert right needle between 6th and 7th sts on left needle and draw loop through, place this loop on left needle and K tog this loop with first st on left needle, K1, P2, K2; **wrap 6 tog** = P1, K4, P1, slip these 6 sts onto cable needle and wrap yarn round these sts 4 times anticlockwise, then slip same 6 sts back onto right needle.

UK CROCHET ABBREVIATIONS

ch = chain; **ss** = slip stitch; **dc** = double crochet.

US CROCHET ABBREVIATIONS

ch = chain; **ss** = slip stitch; **dc** = dsingle crochet.

BACK

Using 9mm (US 13) needles and yarn A cast on 59 [65: 71: 77] sts.
Beg and ending rows as indicated, working chart rows 1 to 11 **once only** and then repeating chart rows 12 to 35 **throughout** and noting that chart row 1 is a **WS** row, cont in patt from chart for back as folls:
Work 11 rows, ending with RS facing for next row.
Dec 1 st at each end of next and foll 4th row.
55 [61: 67: 73] sts.
Work 11 rows, ending with RS facing for next row.
Inc 1 st at each end of next and foll 8th row.
59 [65: 71: 77] sts.
Cont straight until back meas 35 [36: 37: 38] cm, ending with RS facing for next row.

Shape armholes

Keeping patt correct, cast off 4 sts at beg of next 2 rows. 51 [57: 63: 69] sts.
Dec 1 st at each end of next 3 [5: 5: 7] rows, then on foll 1 [1: 2: 2] alt rows.
43 [45: 49: 51] sts.
Cont straight until armhole meas 22 [23: 24: 25] cm, ending with RS facing for next row.

Shape shoulders and back neck

Next row (RS): Cast off 5 [5: 6: 6] sts, patt until there are 8 [9: 9: 10] sts on right needle and turn, leaving rem sts on a holder.
Work each side of neck separately.
Cast off 3 sts at beg of next row.
Cast off rem 5 [6: 6: 7] sts.
With RS facing, rejoin yarn to rem sts, cast off centre 17 [17: 19: 19] sts, patt to end.
Complete to match first side, reversing shapings.

LEFT FRONT

Using 9mm (US 13) needles and yarn A cast on 35 [38: 41: 44] sts.
Beg and ending rows as indicated, working chart rows 1 to 11 **once only** and then repeating chart rows 12 to 35 **throughout** and noting that chart row 1 is a **WS** row, cont in patt from chart for left front as folls:
Work 11 rows, ending with RS facing for next row.
Dec 1 st at beg of next and foll 4th row.
33 [36: 39: 42] sts.
Work 11 rows, ending with RS facing for next row.
Inc 1 st at beg of next and foll 8th row.
35 [38: 41: 44] sts.
Cont straight until left front matches back to beg of armhole shaping, ending with RS facing for next row.

Back chart

Key

☐ K on RS,
  P on WS

▣ P on RS,
  K on WS

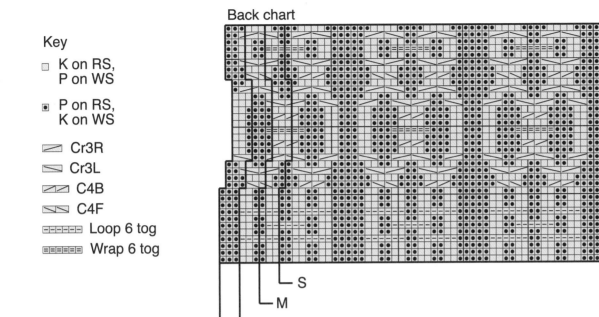

Cr3R
Cr3L
C4B
C4F
Loop 6 tog
Wrap 6 tog

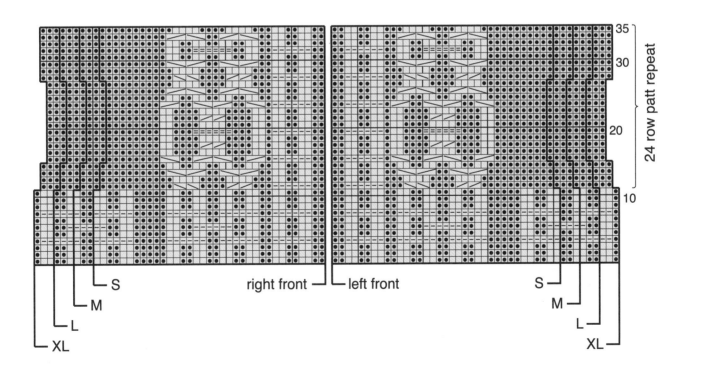

24 row patt repeat

right front left front

Shape armhole

Keeping patt correct, cast off 4 sts at beg of next row.

31 [34: 37: 40] sts.

Work 1 row.

Dec 1 st at armhole edge of next 3 [5: 5: 7] rows, then on foll 1 [1: 2: 2] alt rows.

27 [28: 30: 31] sts.

Cont straight until 9 rows less have been worked than on back to beg of shoulder shaping, ending with **WS** facing for next row.

Shape neck

Keeping patt correct, cast off 12 [12: 13: 13] sts at beg of next row.

15 [16: 17: 18] sts.

Dec 1 st at neck edge of next 3 rows, then on foll 2 alt rows.

10 [11: 12: 13] sts.

Work 1 row, ending with RS facing for next row.

Shape shoulder

Cast off 5 [5: 6: 6] sts at beg of next row.

Work 1 row.

Cast off rem 5 [6: 6: 7] sts.

RIGHT FRONT

Using 9mm (US 13) needles and yarn A cast on

35 [38: 41: 44] sts.

Beg and ending rows as indicated, working chart rows 1 to 11 **once only** and then repeating chart rows 12 to 35 **throughout** and noting that chart row 1 is a **WS** row, cont in patt from chart for right front as folls:

Work 11 rows, ending with RS facing for next row.

Dec 1 st at end of next and foll 4th row.

33 [36: 39: 42] sts.

Complete to match left front, reversing shapings.

SLEEVES

Using 9mm (US 13) needles and yarn A cast on 30 [30: 32: 32] sts.

Beg and ending rows as indicated, working chart rows 1 to 11 **once only** and then repeating chart rows 12 to 35 **throughout** and noting that chart row 1 is a **WS** row, cont in patt from chart for sleeve as folls:

Work 11 rows, ending with RS facing for next row.

Inc 1 st at each end of next and every foll 6th [4th: 6th: 4th] row to 44 [34: 50: 40] sts, then on every foll 8th [6th: -: 6th] row until there are 46 [48: -: 52] sts, taking inc sts into patt.

Cont straight until sleeve meas 44 [45: 46: 46] cm, ending with RS facing for next row.

Shape top

Keeping patt correct, cast off 4 sts at beg of next 2 rows.

38 [40: 42: 44] sts.

Dec 1 st at each end of next and every foll alt row to 24 sts, then on foll 3 rows, ending with RS facing for next row.

Cast off rem 18 sts.

MAKING UP

Press as described on the information page. Join both shoulder seams using back stitch, or mattress stitch if preferred.

Collar

With RS facing, using 9mm (US 13) needles and yarn A, beg and ending at front opening edges, pick up and knit 18 [18: 19: 19] sts up right side of neck, 23 [23: 25: 25] sts from back, then 18 [18: 19: 19] sts down left side of neck.

59 [59: 63: 63] sts.

Row 1 (RS of collar, WS of body): (P2, K2) twice, P3 [3: 4: 4], (P2, K2) 4 times, P3 [3: 5: 5], (P2, K2) 4 times, P3 [3: 4: 4], (P2, K2) twice, P2.

Row 2 and every foll alt row: (K2, P2) twice,

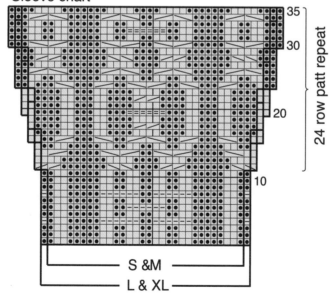

Sleeve chart

35
30
20
10

24 row patt repeat

S & M
L & XL

Key

□ K on RS, P on WS

▣ P on RS, K on WS

⬋ Cr3R

⬊ Cr3L

C4B

C4F

Loop 6 tog

Wrap 6 tog

36

K3 [3: 4: 4], (K2, P2) 4 times, K3 [3: 5: 5], (K2, P2) 4 times, K3 [3: 4: 4], (K2, P2) twice, K2.

Row 3: P2, loop 6 tog, P5 [5: 6: 6], loop 6 tog, P2, loop 6 tog, P5 [5: 7: 7], loop 6 tog, P2, loop 6 tog, P5 [5: 6: 6], loop 6 tog, P2.

Row 5: (P2, K2) twice, P5 [5: 6: 6], K2, P2, loop 6 tog, P2, K2, P5 [5: 7: 7], K2, P2, loop 6 tog, P2, K2, P5 [5: 6: 6], (K2, P2) twice.

Row 6: As row 2.

Rows 3 to 6 form patt.

Cont in patt for a further 10 rows, ending with RS facing for next row.

Rep rows 1 and 2 once more, ending with RS facing for next row.

Cast off in patt.

Crochet edging

With RS facing, using 8.00mm (US L11) crochet hook and yarn B, attach yarn at base of right front opening edge, 1 ch (does NOT count as st), work 1 row of dc evenly up right front opening edge and across cast-off edge of collar to top of left front opening edge, working 1 dc into each cast-off st, turn and work back across cast-off edge of collar as folls: *12 ch, 1 ss into each of next 2 dc, rep from * to last st, 12 ch, 1 ss into last st, turn and work back again along cast-off edge of collar,

working into same dc as worked into for previous row, as folls: *8 ch, 1 ss into each of next 2 dc, rep from * to last st, 8 ch, 1 ss into last st, do NOT turn but cont down left front opening edge in dc to left front cast-on edge.

Fasten off.

See information page for finishing instructions,

setting in sleeves using the set-in method.

Using photograph as a guide and yarn A, make crochet ch button loops and attach buttons to correspond – place lowest button and loop 8 cm up from cast-on edge, top button and loop just below collar pick-up row and rem 3 buttons and loops evenly spaced between.

57 [59: 61: 63] cm
(22½ [23: 24: 25] in)

47 [53: 59: 65] cm
(18½ [21: 23: 25½] in)

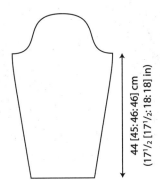

44 [45: 46: 46] cm
(17½ [17½: 18: 18] in)

Main image page 13

SILAS

by MARIE WALLIN

SIZE

	S	M	L	XL	XXL	
To fit chest						
	102	107	112	117	122	cm
	40	42	44	46	48	in

YARN

Rowan Country

A Ash 651

	9	10	11	11	12	x 50gm

B Heather 655

	6	6	7	7	8	x 50gm

NEEDLES

1 pair 8mm (no 0) (US 11) needles
1 pair 9mm (no 00) (US 13) needles

ZIP – open-ended zip to fit

TENSION

11 sts and 18 rows to 10 cm measured over pattern using 9mm (US 13) needles.

SPECIAL ABBREVIATIONS

wyab = with yarn at WS (back on RS rows, front on WS rows) of work.

BACK

Using 8mm (US 11) needles and yarn A cast on 60 [64: 68: 70: 74] sts.
Row 1 (RS): K1 [0: 1: 0: 0], P2 [1: 2: 0: 2], ★K2, P2, rep from ★ to last 1 [3: 1: 2: 0] sts, K1 [2: 1: 2: 0], P0 [1: 0: 0: 0].
Row 2: P1 [0: 1: 0: 0], K2 [1: 2: 0: 2], ★P2, K2, rep from ★ to last 1 [3: 1: 2: 0] sts, P1 [2: 1: 2: 0], K0 [1: 0: 0: 0].
These 2 rows form rib.
Work in rib for a further 8 rows, ending with RS facing for next row.
Change to 9mm (US 13) needles.
Beg and ending rows as indicated and repeating the 24 row patt repeat throughout, cont in patt from chart as folls:
Work straight until back meas 40 [41: 40: 41: 40] cm, ending with RS facing for next row.
Shape armholes
Keeping patt correct, cast off 3 sts at beg of next 2 rows.
54 [58: 62: 64: 68] sts.
Dec 1 st at each end of next 3 rows.
48 [52: 56: 58: 62] sts.
Cont straight until armhole meas 24 [25: 26: 27: 28] cm, ending with RS facing for next row.

Shape shoulders and back neck
Next row (RS): Cast off 6 [7: 8: 8: 9] sts, patt until there are 10 [11: 11: 12: 13] sts on right needle and turn, leaving rem sts on a holder.
Work each side of neck separately.
Cast off 3 sts at beg of next row.
Cast off rem 7 [8: 8: 9: 10] sts.
With RS facing, rejoin yarns to rem sts, cast off centre 16 [16: 18: 18: 18] sts, patt to end.
Complete to match first side, reversing shapings.

LEFT FRONT

Using 8mm (US 11) needles and yarn A cast on 30 [32: 34: 35: 37] sts.
Row 1 (RS): K1 [0: 1: 0: 0], P2 [1: 2: 0: 2], ★K2, P2, rep from ★ to last 3 sts, K2, P1.
Row 2: K1, ★P2, K2, rep from ★ to last 1 [3: 1: 2: 0] sts, P1 [2: 1: 2: 0], K0 [1: 0: 0: 0].
These 2 rows form rib.
Work in rib for a further 8 rows, ending with RS facing for next row.
Change to 9mm (US 13) needles.
Beg and ending rows as indicated, cont in patt from chart as folls:
Work straight until left front matches back to beg of armhole shaping, ending with RS facing for next row.
Shape armhole
Keeping patt correct, cast off 3 sts at beg of next row. 27 [29: 31: 32: 34] sts.
Work 1 row.
Dec 1 st at armhole edge of next 3 rows.
24 [26: 28: 29: 31] sts.
Cont straight until 15 [15: 17: 17: 19] rows less have been worked than on back to beg of shoulder shaping, ending with **WS** facing for next row.
Shape neck
Keeping patt correct, cast off 5 [5: 5: 5: 4] sts at beg of next row.
19 [21: 23: 24: 27] sts.
Dec 1 st at neck edge of next 3 rows, then on foll 2 [2: 3: 3: 4] alt rows, then on foll 4th row.
13 [15: 16: 17: 19] sts.
Work 3 rows, ending with RS facing for next row.
Shape shoulder
Cast off 6 [7: 8: 8: 9] sts at beg of next row.
Work 1 row.
Cast off rem 7 [8: 8: 9: 10] sts.

RIGHT FRONT

Using 8mm (US 11) needles and yarn A cast on

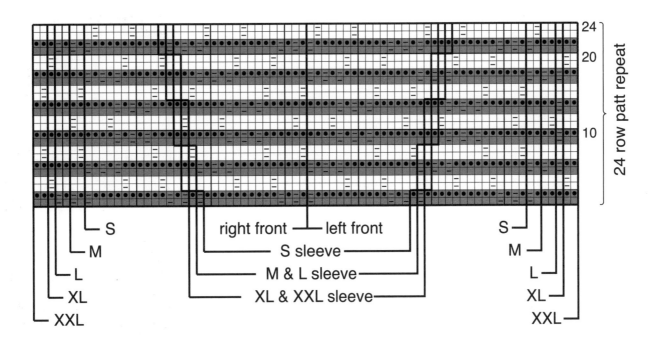

24 row patt repeat

S
M
L
XL
XXL

right front — left front
S sleeve
M & L sleeve
XL & XXL sleeve

S
M
L
XL
XXL

Key

☐ A - K on RS, P on WS

⊡ A - P on RS, K on WS

▪ B - K on RS, P on WS

▣ B - P on RS, K on WS

⊟ Slip st wyib

---

30 [32: 34: 35: 37] sts.
Row 1 (RS): P1, *K2, P2, rep from * to last 1 [3: 1: 2: 0] sts, K1 [2: 1: 2: 0], P0 [1: 0: 0: 0].
Row 2: P1 [0: 1: 0: 0], K2 [1: 2: 0: 2], *P2, K2, rep from * to last 3 sts, P2, K1.
These 2 rows form rib.
Complete to match left front, reversing shapings.

SLEEVES
Using 8mm (US 11) needles and yarn A cast on 28 [30: 30: 32: 32] sts.
Row 1 (RS): K1 [0: 0: 0: 0], P2 [0: 0: 1: 1], *K2, P2, rep from * to last 1 [2: 2: 3: 3] sts, K1 [2: 2: 2: 2], P0 [0: 0: 1: 1].
Row 2: P1 [0: 0: 0: 0], K2 [0: 0: 1: 1], *P2, K2, rep from * to last 1 [2: 2: 3: 3] sts, P1 [2: 2: 2: 2],

K0 [0: 0: 1: 1].
These 2 rows form rib.
Work in rib for a further 8 rows, ending with RS facing for next row.
Change to 9mm (US 13) needles.
Beg and ending rows as indicated, cont in patt from chart, shaping sides by inc 1 st at each end of 3rd and every foll 6th row to 46 [44: 56: 54: 58] sts, then on every foll 8th row until there are 52 [54: 58: 60: 62] sts, taking inc sts into patt.
Cont straight until sleeve meas 52 [54: 56: 58: 60] cm, ending with RS facing for next row.
Shape top
Keeping patt correct, cast off 3 sts at beg of next 2 rows.
46 [48: 52: 54: 56] sts.

Dec 1 st at each end of next and foll 2 alt rows, then on foll row, ending with RS facing for next row.
Cast off rem 38 [40: 44: 46: 48] sts.

MAKING UP
Press as described on the information page.
Join both shoulder seams using back stitch, or mattress stitch if preferred.
Collar
With RS facing, using 8mm (US 11) needles and yarn A, beg and ending at front opening edges, pick up and knit 22 [22: 23: 23: 25] sts up right side of neck, 22 [22: 24: 24: 24] sts from back, then 22 [22: 23: 23: 25] sts down left side of neck.
66 [66: 70: 70: 74] sts.

Row 1 (WS): P2, *K2, P2, rep from * to end.
Row 2: K2, *P2, K2, rep from * to end.
Rep last 2 rows until collar meas 10 cm, ending with RS facing for next row.
Cast off in rib.

Front bands (both alike)

With RS facing, using 8mm (US 11) needles and yarn A, pick up and knit 65 [67: 67: 67: 67] sts along front opening edge, between cast-on edge and top of collar.

Row 1 (WS): P1, *K1, P1, rep from * to end.
Row 2: K1, *P1, K1, rep from * to end.
Cast off in rib (on **WS**).

See information page for finishing instructions, setting in sleeves using the shallow set-in method.

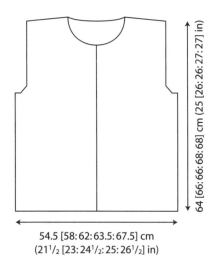

64 [66: 66: 68: 68] cm (25 [26: 26: 27: 27] in)

54.5 [58: 62: 63.5: 67.5] cm
(21^1/$_2$ [23: 24^1/$_2$: 25: 26^1/$_2$] in)

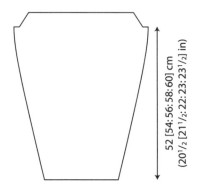

52 [54: 56: 58: 60] cm
(20^1/$_2$ [21^1/$_2$: 22: 23: 23^1/$_2$] in)

Main image page 11

MORRIGAN

by MARIE WALLIN

SIZE

	S	M	L	XL	XXL	
To fit chest						
	102	107	112	117	122	cm
	40	42	44	46	48	in

YARN

Rowan Country

A Willow 652

9	10	10	11	11	x 50gm

B Ash 651

5	5	5	5	6	x 50gm

C Reed 659

3	3	3	3	3	x 50gm

D Juniper 654

3	4	4	4	4	x 50gm

NEEDLES

1 pair 8mm (no 0) (US 11) needles
1 pair 9mm (no 00) (US 13) needles

BUTTONS – 5 x 00410

TENSION

10 sts and 17 rows to 10 cm measured over pattern using 9mm (US 13) needles.

BACK

Using 8mm (US 11) needles and yarn A cast on 61 [63: 67: 69: 73] sts.
Row 1 (RS): K1, *P1, K1, rep from * to end.
Row 2: P1, *K1, P1, rep from * to end.
These 2 rows form rib.
Work in rib for a further 8 rows, ending with RS facing for next row.
Change to 9mm (US 13) needles.
Beg and ending rows as indicated and repeating the 38 row patt repeat throughout, cont in patt from chart as folls:
Work straight until back meas 45 [46: 45: 46: 45] cm, ending with RS facing for next row.
Shape armholes
Keeping patt correct, cast off 3 sts at beg of next 2 rows.
55 [57: 61: 63: 67] sts.
Dec 1 st at each end of next 3 rows.
49 [51: 55: 57: 61] sts.
Cont straight until armhole meas 25 [26: 27: 28: 29] cm, ending with RS facing for next row.
Shape shoulders and back neck
Next row (RS): Cast off 7 [8: 8: 9: 10] sts, patt until there are 11 [11: 12: 12: 13] sts on right needle and turn, leaving rem sts on a holder.

Work each side of neck separately.
Cast off 3 sts at beg of next row.
Cast off rem 8 [8: 9: 9: 10] sts.
With RS facing, rejoin yarns to rem sts, cast off centre 13 [13: 15: 15: 15] sts, patt to end.
Complete to match first side, reversing shapings.

LEFT FRONT

Using 8mm (US 11) needles and yarn A cast on 30 [32: 34: 34: 36] sts.
Row 1 (RS): *K1, P1, rep from * to end.
Row 2: As row 1.
These 2 rows form rib.
Work in rib for a further 8 rows, inc 1 [0: 0: 1: 1] st at end of last row and ending with RS facing for next row.
31 [32: 34: 35: 37] sts.
Change to 9mm (US 13) needles.
Beg and ending rows as indicated, cont in patt from chart as folls:
Work straight until left front matches back to beg of armhole shaping, ending with RS facing for next row.
Shape armhole
Keeping patt correct, cast off 3 sts at beg of next row.
28 [29: 31: 32: 34] sts.
Work 1 row.
Dec 1 st at armhole edge of next 3 rows.
25 [26: 28: 29: 31] sts.
Cont straight until 13 [13: 15: 15: 17] rows less have been worked than on back to beg of shoulder shaping, ending with **WS** facing for next row.
Shape neck
Keeping patt correct, cast off 5 [5: 5: 5: 4] sts at beg of next row.
20 [21: 23: 24: 27] sts.
Dec 1 st at neck edge of next 3 rows, then on foll 2 [2: 3: 3: 4] alt rows.
15 [16: 17: 18: 20] sts.
Work 5 rows, ending with RS facing for next row.
Shape shoulder
Cast off 7 [8: 8: 9: 10] sts at beg of next row.
Work 1 row.
Cast off rem 8 [8: 9: 9: 10] sts.

RIGHT FRONT

Using 8mm (US 11) needles and yarn A cast on 30 [32: 34: 34: 36] sts.
Row 1 (RS): *P1, K1, rep from * to end.
Row 2: As row 1.

These 2 rows form rib.
Work in rib for a further 8 rows, inc 1 [0: 0: 1: 1] st at beg of last row and ending with RS facing for next row.
31 [32: 34: 35: 37] sts.
Complete to match left front, reversing shapings.

SLEEVES

Using 8mm (US 11) needles and yarn A cast on 29 [31: 31: 33: 33] sts.
Work in rib as given for back for 10 rows, ending with RS facing for next row.
Change to 9mm (US 13) needles.
Beg and ending rows as indicated, cont in patt from chart, shaping sides by inc 1 st at each end of 3rd and every foll 6th row to 49 [49: 53: 51: 57] sts, then on every foll 8th row until there are 51 [53: 55: 57: 59] sts, taking inc sts into patt.
Cont straight until sleeve meas 48 [50: 52: 54: 56] cm, ending with RS facing for next row.
Shape top
Keeping patt correct, cast off 3 sts at beg of next 2 rows.
45 [47: 49: 51: 53] sts.
Dec 1 st at each end of next and foll 2 alt rows, then on foll row, ending with RS facing for next row.
Cast off rem 37 [39: 41: 43: 45] sts.

MAKING UP

Press as described on the information page.
Join both shoulder seams using back stitch, or mattress stitch if preferred.
Button band
With RS facing, using 8mm (US 11) needles and yarn A, pick up and knit 63 [63: 63: 67: 67] sts up right front opening edge, from cast-on edge to neck shaping.
Beg with row 2, work in rib as given for back for 6 rows, ending with **WS** facing for next row.
Cast off in rib (on **WS**).
Buttonhole band
With RS facing, using 8mm (US 11) needles and yarn A, pick up and knit 63 [63: 63: 67: 67] sts down left front opening edge, from neck shaping to cast-on edge.
Beg with row 2, work in rib as given for back for 3 rows, ending with RS facing for next row.
Row 4 (RS): rib 3, *yrn (to make a buttonhole), work 2 tog, rib 12 [12: 12: 13: 13], rep from * 3 times more, yrn (to make 5th buttonhole), work 2 tog, rib 2.

Work in rib for a further 2 rows, ending with **WS** facing for next row.
Cast off in rib (on **WS**).

Collar
With RS facing, using 8mm (US 11) needles and yarn A, beg and ending halfway across top of bands, pick up and knit 23 [23: 24: 24: 26] sts up right side of neck, 19 [19: 21: 21: 21] sts from back, then 23 [23: 24: 24: 26] sts down left side of neck.
65 [65: 69: 69: 73] sts.
Beg with row 1, work in rib as given for back for 10 cm, ending with RS of body (**WS** of collar) facing for next row.
Next row (WS of collar): rib 4, *inc in next st, rib 3, rep from * to last st, rib 1.
80 [80: 85: 85: 90] sts.
Next row: (K1, P1) twice, *K2, P1, K1, P1, rep from * to last st, K1.
Next row: (P1, K1) twice, *P2, K1, P1, K1, rep

from * to last st, P1.
Rep last 2 rows until collar meas 18 cm, ending with RS of collar facing for next row.

Cast off in patt.
See information page for finishing instructions, setting in sleeves using the shallow set-in method.

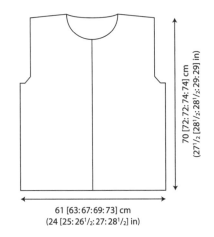

70 [72: 72: 74: 74] cm
(27½ [28½: 28½: 29: 29] in)

61 [63: 67: 69: 73] cm
(24 [25: 26½: 27: 28½] in)

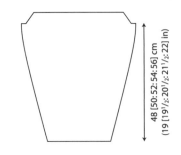

48 [50: 52: 54: 56] cm
(19 [19½: 20½: 21½: 22] in)

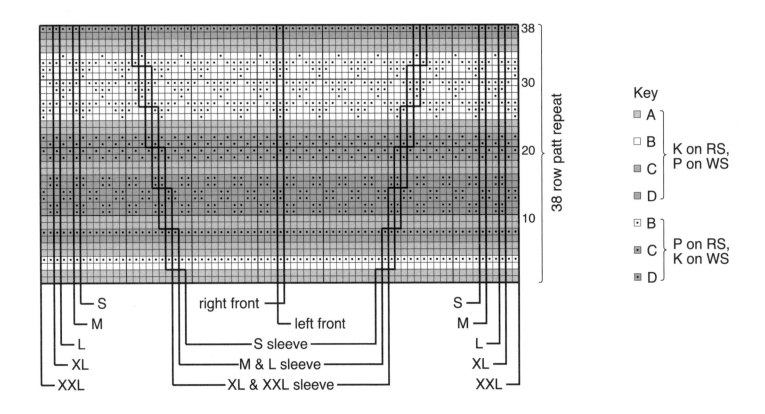

38 row patt repeat

S
M
L
XL
XXL

right front
left front
S sleeve
M & L sleeve
XL & XXL sleeve

S
M
L
XL
XXL

Key

▨ A
☐ B
▨ C
▨ D
} K on RS, P on WS

⊡ B
▪ C
▪ D
} P on RS, K on WS

Main image page 10

AILISH BAG

by MARIE WALLIN

YARN
Rowan Country

A Birch 650	9	x 50gm
B Cedarwood 653	2	x 50gm
C Ash 651	2	x 50gm

NEEDLES
1 pair 8mm (no 0) (US 11) needles
8.00mm (no 0) (US L11) crochet hook

TENSION
10 sts and 6 rows to 10 cm measured over treble fabric using 8.00mm (US L11) crochet hook.

UK CROCHET ABBREVIATIONS
ch = chain; **dc** = double crochet; **tr** = treble.

US CROCHET ABBREVIATIONS
ch = chain; **dc** = single crochet; **tr** = double.

FINISHED SIZE
Completed bag measures 35 cm (14 in) wide and 35 cm (14 in) deep.

FLAP AND BACK
Using 8.00mm (US L11) crochet hook and yarn A make 36 ch.
Row 1 (RS): 1 dc into 2nd ch from hook, 1 dc into each ch to end, turn. 35 sts.
Row 2: 3 ch (counts as first tr), miss dc at base of 3 ch, 1 tr into each dc to end, turn.
Row 3: 3 ch (counts as first tr), miss tr at base of 3 ch, 1 tr into each tr to end, working last tr into top of 3 ch at beg of previous row, turn.
Row 3 forms patt.★★
Cont in patt until work meas 25 cm.
Place markers at both ends of last row to denote top of back.
Cont in patt until work meas 60 cm – this last section forms back.
Fasten off.

FRONT
Work as given for flap and back to ★★.
Cont in patt until front meas 35 cm.
Fasten off.
Place markers at both ends of last row to denote top of front.

STRAP AND GUSSET
Using 8.00mm (US L11) crochet hook and yarn A make 202 ch.
Row 1 (RS): 1 dc into 2nd ch from hook, 1 dc into each ch to end, turn. 201 sts.
Row 2: 3 ch (counts as first tr), miss dc at base of 3 ch, 1 tr into each dc to end, turn.
Row 3: 3 ch (counts as first tr), miss tr at base of 3 ch, 1 tr into each tr to end, working last tr into top of 3 ch at beg of previous row, turn.
Rows 4 to 7: As row 3.
Fasten off.
Place markers along both long edges, 53 cm away from both short edges (4 markers in total).

MAKING UP
Press as described on the information page.
Embroidery
Using photograph as a guide and yarn B DOUBLE, work a row of cross stitch over rows 3 and 4 of flap section. Leave 2 rows, then work another row of cross stitch over next 2 rows. Cont in this way until entire flap and back section are embroidered, ensuring there are 2 rows of crochet between each row of cross stitch. Embroider cross stitch lines onto front in same way.
Using yarn B DOUBLE, embroider a line of running stitch across flap where rows 5 and 6 join – this should be midway between lines of cross stitch. Using yarn C DOUBLE, thread this yarn under line of running stitch to form a wavy line sitting on surface of crochet. Cont in this way, working lines of running stitch in yarn B decorated with wavy lines in yarn C, until all gaps between cross stitch lines on flap, back and front are filled. Now work a line of running stitch in yarn B decorated with wavy lines in yarn C centrally along strap and gusset.
Join row end edges of strap and gusset. Positioning gusset seam at centre of foundation ch of front and at centre of last row of back, and matching markers on gusset to markers on back and front, sew strap and gusset to back and front.
Tassel strip
With RS facing and using 8.00mm (US L11) crochet hook, attach yarn A to centre of foundation ch of flap, 6 ch, ★slip loop on crochet hook onto 8mm (US 11) knitting needle and work (K into front, back, front, back and front again) into this st, (turn and P5, turn and K5) twice, lift 2nd, 3rd, 4th and 5th sts on right needle over first st and off right needle, slip this st onto 8.00mm (US L11) crochet hook and make 3 ch, rep from ★ once more.
Fasten off.
Using yarn A, run a gathering thread around each bobble on ch and pull up tight. Fasten off securely. Using yarn A, make a 12 cm long tassel and attach to end of chain.

WOODLAND

by MARIE WALLIN

SIZE

8	10	12	14	16	18	20	22	

To fit bust

82	87	92	97	102	107	112	117	cm
32	34	36	38	40	42	44	46	in

YARN

Rowan Country

11	11	12	12	13	14	14	15	x 50gm

(photographed in Ash 651)

NEEDLES

1 pair 8mm (no 0) (US 11) needles
1 pair 9mm (no 00) (US 13) needles
8mm (no 0) (US 11) circular needle

RIBBON – 2.50 m of 25 mm wide organza ribbon

TENSION

10 sts and 14 rows to 10 cm measured over stocking stitch using 9mm (US 13) needles.

SPECIAL ABBREVIATIONS

MB = (K1, P1, K1) all into next st, turn and P3, turn and K3, turn and P3, turn, lift 2nd and 3rd sts on left needle over first st and off left needle, K1.

BACK

Using 8mm (US 11) needles cast on 46 [48: 50: 54: 56: 60: 62: 66] sts.
Row 1 (RS): K0 [1: 0: 0: 1: 0: 0: 0], P2 [2: 0: 2: 2: 1: 2: 0], *K2, P2, rep from * to last 0 [1: 2: 0: 1: 3: 0: 2] sts, K0 [1: 2: 0: 1: 2: 0: 2], P0 [0: 0: 0: 0: 1: 0: 0].
Row 2: P0 [1: 0: 0: 1: 0: 0: 0], K2 [2: 0: 2: 2: 1: 2: 0], *P2, K2, rep from * to last 0 [1: 2: 0: 1: 3: 0: 2] sts, P0 [1: 2: 0: 1: 2: 0: 2], K0 [0: 0: 0: 0: 1: 0: 0].
These 2 rows form rib.
Work in rib for a further 8 rows, dec 1 st at end of last row and ending with RS facing for next row.
45 [47: 49: 53: 55: 59: 61: 65] sts.
Change to 9mm (US 13) needles.
Row 1 (RS): Knit.
Row 2: Purl.
Row 3: K2 [3: 4: 2: 3: 1: 2: 4], MB, *K3, MB, rep from * to last 2 [3: 4: 2: 3: 1: 2: 4] sts, K2 [3: 4: 2: 3: 1: 2: 4].
Row 4: Purl.
Row 5: K4 [1: 2: 4: 1: 3: 4: 2], MB, *K3, MB, rep from * to last 4 [1: 2: 4: 1: 3: 4: 2] sts, K4 [1: 2: 4: 1: 3: 4: 2].

Beg with a P row, cont in st st until back meas 21 [21: 20: 23: 22: 24: 23: 25] cm, ending with RS facing for next row.
Dec 1 st at each end of next row.
43 [45: 47: 51: 53: 57: 59: 63] sts.
Work 17 rows, ending with RS facing for next row. (Back should meas 34 [34: 33: 36: 35: 37: 36: 38] cm.)

Shape armholes
Cast off 2 sts at beg of next 2 rows.
39 [41: 43: 47: 49: 53: 55: 59] sts.
Dec 1 st at each end of next 3 [3: 3: 5: 5: 5: 5: 5] rows, then on foll 0 [0: 0: 0: 0: 2: 2: 3] alt rows.
33 [35: 37: 37: 39: 39: 41: 43] sts.
Cont straight until armhole meas 21 [21: 22: 22: 23: 23: 24: 24] cm, ending with RS facing for next row.

Shape shoulders and back neck
Next row (RS): Cast off 2 [3: 3: 3: 3: 3: 4: 4] sts, K until there are 6 [6: 7: 7: 7: 7: 7: 8] sts on right needle and turn, leaving rem sts on a holder.
Work each side of neck separately.
Cast off 3 sts at beg of next row.
Cast off rem 3 [3: 4: 4: 4: 4: 4: 5] sts.
With RS facing, rejoin yarn to rem sts, cast off centre 17 [17: 17: 17: 19: 19: 19: 19] sts, K to end.
Complete to match first side, reversing shapings.

LEFT FRONT

Using 8mm (US 11) needles cast on 21 [22: 23: 25: 26: 28: 29: 31] sts.
Row 1 (RS): K0 [1: 0: 0: 1: 0: 0: 0], P2 [2: 0: 2: 2: 1: 2: 0], *K2, P2, rep from * to last 3 sts, K2, P1.
Row 2: K1, *P2, K2, rep from * to last 0 [1: 2: 0: 1: 3: 0: 2] sts, P0 [1: 2: 0: 1: 2: 0: 2], K0 [0: 0: 0: 0: 1: 0: 0].
These 2 rows form rib.
Work in rib for a further 8 rows, ending with RS facing for next row.
Change to 9mm (US 13) needles.
Row 1 (RS): Knit.
Row 2: Purl.
Row 3: K2 [3: 4: 2: 3: 1: 2: 4], MB, *K3, MB, rep from * to last 2 sts, K2.
Row 4: Purl.
Row 5: K4 [1: 2: 4: 1: 3: 4: 2], MB, *K3, MB, rep from * to last 4 sts, K4.
Row 6: Purl.
Row 7: K to last 3 sts, MB, K2.
Rows 6 and 7 set the sts.
Keeping sts correct, cont as now set until left front meas 21 [21: 20: 23: 22: 24: 23: 25] cm, ending

with RS facing for next row.
Dec 1 st at beg of next row.
20 [21: 22: 24: 25: 27: 28: 30] sts.
Work 3 rows, ending with RS facing for next row.

Shape front slope
Next row (RS): K to last 5 sts, K2tog, MB, K2.
Working all front slope shaping as set by last row, dec 1 st at front slope edge of 4th and every foll 4th row until 16 [17: 18: 20: 21: 23: 24: 26] sts rem.
Work 1 row, ending with RS facing for next row.

Shape armhole
Cast off 2 sts at beg of next row.
14 [15: 16: 18: 19: 21: 22: 24] sts.
Work 1 row.
Dec 1 st at armhole edge of next 3 [3: 3: 5: 5: 5: 5: 5] rows, then on foll 0 [0: 0: 0: 0: 2: 2: 3] alt rows **and at same time** dec 1 st at front slope edge of next and every foll 0 [0: 0: 4th: 4th: 4th: 4th: 4th] row. 10 [11: 12: 11: 12: 11: 12: 13] sts.
Dec 1 st at front slope edge **only** of 2nd [2nd: 2nd: 4th: 4th: 4th: 4th: 2nd] and 3 [3: 3: 2: 4: 3: 2: 2] foll 4th rows, then on foll 6th [6th: 6th: 6th: 0: 0: 6th: 6th] row. 5 [6: 7: 7: 7: 7: 8: 9] sts.
Cont straight until left front matches back to beg of shoulder shaping, ending with RS facing for next row.

Shape shoulder
Cast off 2 [3: 3: 3: 3: 3: 4: 4] sts at beg of next row.
Work 1 row.
Cast off rem 3 [3: 4: 4: 4: 4: 4: 5] sts.

RIGHT FRONT
Using 8mm (US 11) needles cast on 21 [22: 23: 25: 26: 28: 29: 31] sts.
Row 1 (RS): P1, *K2, P2, rep from * to last 0 [1: 2: 0: 1: 3: 0: 2] sts, K0 [1: 2: 0: 1: 2: 0: 2], P0 [0: 0: 0: 0: 1: 0: 0].
Row 2: P0 [1: 0: 0: 1: 0: 0: 0], K2 [2: 0: 2: 2: 1: 2: 0], *P2, K2, rep from * to last 3 sts, P2, K1.
These 2 rows form rib.
Work in rib for a further 8 rows, ending with RS facing for next row.
Change to 9mm (US 13) needles.
Row 1 (RS): Knit.
Row 2: Purl.
Row 3: K2, MB, *K3, MB, rep from * to last 2 [3: 4: 2: 3: 1: 2: 4] sts, K2 [3: 4: 2: 3: 1: 2: 4].
Row 4: Purl.
Row 5: K4, MB, *K3, MB, rep from * to last 4 [1: 2: 4: 1: 3: 4: 2] sts, K4 [1: 2: 4: 1: 3: 4: 2].
Row 6: Purl.

Row 7: K2, MB, K to end.
Rows 6 and 7 set the sts.
Keeping sts correct, cont as now set until right front meas 21 [21: 20: 23: 22: 24: 23: 25] cm, ending with RS facing for next row.
Dec 1 st at end of next row.
20 [21: 22: 24: 25: 27: 28: 30] sts.
Work 3 rows, ending with RS facing for next row.

Shape front slope
Next row (RS): K2, MB, sl 1, K1, psso, K to end.
Working all front slope shaping as set by last row, complete to match left front, reversing shapings.

SLEEVES
Using 8mm (US 11) needles cast on 28 [28: 30: 30: 32: 32: 34: 34] sts.
Row 1 (RS): K1 [1: 0: 0: 0: 0: 0: 0], P2 [2: 0: 0: 1: 1: 2: 2], *K2, P2, rep from * to last 1 [1: 2: 2: 3: 3: 0: 0] sts, K1 [1: 2: 2: 2: 2: 0: 0], P0 [0: 0: 0: 1: 1: 0: 0].
Row 2: P1 [1: 0: 0: 0: 0: 0: 0], K2 [2: 0: 0: 1: 1: 2: 2], *P2, K2, rep from * to last 1 [1: 2: 2: 3: 3: 0: 0] sts, P1 [1: 2: 2: 2: 2: 0: 0], K0 [0: 0: 0: 1: 1: 0: 0].
These 2 rows form rib.
Work in rib for a further 8 rows, dec 1 st at end of last row and ending with RS facing for next row.
27 [27: 29: 29: 31: 31: 33: 33] sts.
Change to 9mm (US 13) needles.
Row 1 (RS): Knit.
Row 2: Purl.
Row 3: Inc in first st, K0 [0: 1: 1: 2: 2: 3: 3], *K3, MB, rep from * to last 1 [1: 2: 2: 3: 3: 4: 4] sts, K0 [0: 1: 1: 2: 2: 3: 3], inc in last st.
29 [29: 31: 31: 33: 33: 35: 35] sts.
Row 4: Purl.
Row 5: K4 [4: 1: 1: 2: 2: 3: 3], MB, *K3, MB, rep from * to last 4 [4: 1: 1: 2: 2: 3: 3] sts, K4 [4: 1: 1: 2: 2: 3: 3].
Beg with a P row, cont in st st, shaping sides by inc 1 st at each end of 4th and every foll 6th row to 35 [35: 37: 37: 37: 37: 41: 41] sts, then on every foll 8th row until there are 41 [41: 43: 43: 45: 45: 47: 47] sts.
Cont straight until sleeve meas 43 [43: 44: 44: 45: 45: 44: 44] cm, ending with RS facing for next row.

Shape top
Cast off 2 sts at beg of next 2 rows.
37 [37: 39: 39: 41: 41: 43: 43] sts.
Dec 1 st at each end of next 5 rows, then on every foll alt row to 21 sts, then on foll 5 rows, ending

with RS facing for next row. 11 sts.
Cast off 2 sts at beg of next 2 rows.
Cast off rem 7 sts.

MAKING UP
Press as described on the information page.
Join both shoulder seams using back stitch, or mattress stitch if preferred.

Front band
With RS facing and using 8mm (US 11) circular needle, beg and ending at cast-on edges, pick up and knit 32 [32: 31: 35: 34: 36: 35: 37] sts up right front opening edge to beg of front slope shaping, 36 [36: 37: 37: 38: 38: 39: 39] sts up right front slope, 22 [22: 22: 22: 26: 26: 26: 26] sts from back,

55 [55: 55: 58: 58: 60: 60: 62] cm
(21½ [21½: 21½: 23: 23: 23½: 23½: 24½] in)

43 [45: 47: 51: 53: 57: 59: 63] cm
(17 [17½: 18½: 20: 21: 22½: 23: 25] in)

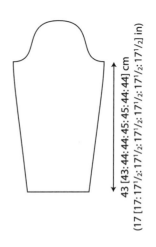

43 [43: 44: 44: 45: 45: 44: 44] cm
(17 [17: 17½: 17½: 17½: 17½: 17½: 17½] in)

45

36 [36: 37: 37: 38: 38: 39: 39] sts down left front slope to beg of front slope shaping, then 32 [32: 31: 35: 34: 36: 35: 37] sts down left front opening edge. 158 [158: 158: 166: 170: 174: 174: 178] sts.
Row 1 (WS): P2, *K2, P2, rep from * to end.

Row 2: K2, *P2, K2, rep from * to end.
These 2 rows form rib.
Work in rib for a further 5 rows, ending with RS facing for next row.
Cast off in rib.

See information page for finishing instructions, setting in sleeves using the set-in method.
Using photograph as a guide, thread ribbon through fronts and back 4 cm below beg of front slope shaping.

Main image page 6 & 19

■ ■

BRANWEN

by MARIE WALLIN

SIZE

8	10	12	14	16	18	
To fit bust						
82	87	92	97	102	107	cm
32	34	36	38	40	42	in

YARN
Rowan Country and Felted Tweed
A Country Heather 655

9	9	10	10	11	11	x 50gm

B Felted Tweed Dragon 147

1	1	1	1	1	1	x 50gm

C Felted Tweed Cocoa 143

1	1	1	1	1	1	x 50gm

D Felted Tweed Camel 157

1	1	1	1	1	1	x 50gm

NEEDLES
1 pair 8mm (no 0) (US 11) needles
1 pair 9mm (no 00) (US 13) needles
4.00mm (no 8) (US G6) crochet hook

TENSION
10 sts and 14 rows to 10 cm measured over stocking stitch using 9mm (US 13) needles and yarn A.

UK CROCHET ABBREVIATIONS
ch = chain; **dc** = double crochet; **sp** = space; **ss** = slip stitch; **tr** = treble; **ttr4tog** = *yoh 3 times and insert hook as indicated, yoh and draw loop through, (yoh and draw through 2 loops) 3 times, rep from * 3 times more, yoh and draw through all 5 loops on hook; **ttr5tog** = *yoh 3 times and insert hook as indicated, yoh and draw loop through, (yoh and draw through 2 loops) 3 times, rep from * 4 times more, yoh and draw through all 6 loops on hook; **yoh** = yarn over hook.

US CROCHET ABBREVIATIONS
ch = chain; **dc** = single crochet; **sp** = space; **ss** = slip stitch; **tr** =double; **ttr4tog** = *yoh 3 times and insert hook as indicated, yoh and draw loop through, (yoh and draw through 2 loops) 3 times, rep from * 3 times more, yoh and draw through all 5 loops on hook; **ttr5tog** = *yoh 3 times and insert hook as indicated, yoh and draw loop through, (yoh and draw through 2 loops) 3 times, rep from * 4 times more, yoh and draw through all 6 loops on hook; **yoh** = yarn over hook.

BACK
Using 8mm (US 11) needles and yarn A cast on 42 [44: 46: 50: 52: 56] sts.
Row 1 (RS): K0 [1: 0: 0: 1: 0], P2 [2: 0: 2: 2: 1], *K2, P2, rep from * to last 0 [1: 2: 0: 1: 3] sts, K0 [1: 2: 0: 1: 2], P0 [0: 0: 0: 0: 1].
Row 2: P0 [1: 0: 0: 1: 0], K2 [2: 0: 2: 2: 1], *P2, K2, rep from * to last 0 [1: 2: 0: 1: 3] sts, P0 [1: 2: 0: 1: 2], K0 [0: 0: 0: 0: 1].
These 2 rows form rib.
Work in rib for a further 10 rows, ending with RS facing for next row.
Change to 9mm (US 13) needles.
Beg with a K row, work in st st, shaping side seams by dec 1 st at each end of 3rd and foll 4th row.
38 [40: 42: 46: 48: 52] sts.
Work 5 rows, ending with RS facing for next row.
Inc 1 st at each end of next and foll 10th row.
42 [44: 46: 50: 52: 56] sts.
Cont straight until back meas 34 [34: 33: 36: 35: 37] cm, ending with RS facing for next row.
Shape armholes
Cast off 2 sts at beg of next 2 rows.

38 [40: 42: 46: 48: 52] sts.
Dec 1 st at each end of next 2 [3: 3: 4: 5: 6] rows.
34 [34: 36: 38: 38: 40] sts.
Cont straight until armhole meas 20 [20: 21: 21: 22: 22] cm, ending with RS facing for next row.
Shape shoulders and back neck
Next row (RS): Cast off 4 [4: 5: 5: 5: 5] sts, K until there are 8 [8: 8: 9: 8: 9] sts on right needle and turn, leaving rem sts on a holder.
Work each side of neck separately.
Cast off 3 sts at beg of next row.
Cast off rem 5 [5: 5: 6: 5: 6] sts.
With RS facing, rejoin yarn to rem sts, cast off centre 10 [10: 10: 10: 12: 12] sts, K to end.
Complete to match first side, reversing shapings.

FRONT
Work as given for back until 10 rows less have been worked than on back to beg of shoulder shaping, ending with RS facing for next row.
Shape neck
Next row (RS): K12 [12: 13: 14: 13: 14] and turn, leaving rem sts on a holder.
Work each side of neck separately.
Dec 1 st at neck edge of next 2 rows, then on foll alt row. 9 [9: 10: 11: 10: 11] sts.
Work 5 rows, ending with RS facing for next row.
Shape shoulder
Cast off 4 [4: 5: 5: 5: 5] sts at beg of next row.
Work 1 row.
Cast off rem 5 [5: 5: 6: 5: 6] sts.
With RS facing, rejoin yarn to rem sts, cast off centre 10 [10: 10: 10: 12: 12] sts, K to end.
Complete to match first side, reversing shapings.

SLEEVES
Using 8mm (US 11) needles and yarn A cast on 22 [22: 24: 24: 26: 26] sts.
Row 1 (RS): P0 [0: 1: 1: 2: 2], *K2, P2, rep from * to last 2 [2: 3: 3: 4: 4] sts, K2, P0 [0: 1: 1: 2: 2].
Row 2: K0 [0: 1: 1: 2: 2], *P2, K2, rep from * to last 2 [2: 3: 3: 4: 4] sts, P2, K0 [0: 1: 1: 2: 2].
These 2 rows form rib.
Work in rib for a further 10 rows, inc 1 st at each end of 5th of these rows and ending with RS facing for next row. 24 [24: 26: 26: 28: 28] sts.
Change to 9mm (US 13) needles.
Beg with a K row, work in st st, shaping side seams by inc 1 st at each end of next and every foll 6th row to 32 [32: 34: 34: 34: 34] sts, then on every foll 8th row until there are 38 [38: 40: 40: 42: 42] sts.

Cont straight until sleeve meas 43 [43: 44: 44: 45: 45] cm, ending with RS facing for next row.
Shape top
Cast off 2 sts at beg of next 2 rows.
34 [34: 36: 36: 38: 38] sts.
Dec 1 st at each end of next 5 rows, then on every foll alt row to 16 sts, then on foll 5 rows, ending with RS facing for next row.
Cast off rem 6 sts.

MAKING UP
Press as described on the information page.
Join right shoulder seam using back stitch, or mattress stitch if preferred.
Neckband
With RS facing, using 8mm (US 11) needles and yarn A, pick up and knit 10 sts down left side of neck, 10 [10: 10: 10: 12: 12] sts from front, 10 sts up right side of neck, then 16 [16: 16: 16: 18: 18] sts from back.
46 [46: 46: 46: 50: 50] sts.
Row 1 (WS): P2, *K2, P2, rep from * to end.
Row 2: K2, *P2, K2, rep from * to end.
These 2 rows form rib.
Cont in rib until neckband meas 7 cm, ending with RS facing for next row.
Cast off in rib.
See information page for finishing instructions, setting in sleeves using the set-in method.
Large motifs (make 5 in total)
Using 4.00mm (US G6) crochet hook and yarn B make 5 ch and join with a ss to form a ring.
Round 1 (WS): 3 ch (counts as first tr), 15 tr into ring, ss to top of 3 ch at beg of round. 16 sts.
Round 2: 1 ch (does NOT count as st), 2 dc between 3 ch at beg of previous round and next tr, *miss 1 tr, 2 dc between tr just missed and next tr, rep from * to end, ss to first dc. 32 sts.
Round 3: 5 ch (does NOT count as st), miss first dc, ttr4 tog over next 4 dc, *9 ch, ttr5tog over dc just worked into and next 4 dc, rep from * to end, 9 ch, ss to top of ttr4tog at beg of round.
Round 4: 1 ch (does NOT count as st), 9 dc into each ch sp to end, ss to first dc. 72 sts.
Fasten off.
Make a further 4 large motifs – one more using yarn B, one using yarn C and 2 using yarn D.
Medium motifs (make 3 in total)
Using 4.00mm (US G6) crochet hook and yarn B make 6 ch and join with a ss to form a ring.
Round 1 (WS): 3 ch (counts as first tr), 15 tr into ring, ss to top of 3 ch at beg of round. 16 sts.

Round 2: 5 ch (counts as first tr and 2 ch), 1 tr into st at base of 5 ch, *1 ch, miss 1 tr**, (1 tr, 2 ch and 1 tr) into next tr, rep from * to end, ending last rep at **, ss to 3rd of 5 ch at beg of round.
Round 3: ss along and into first 2-ch sp, 3 ch (counts as first tr), (1 tr, 2 ch and 2 tr) into same ch sp, *1 ch, miss (1 tr, 1 ch and 1 tr)**, (2 tr, 2 ch and 2 tr) into next ch sp, rep from * to end, ending last rep at **, ss to top of 3 ch at beg of round.
Fasten off.
Make a further 2 medium motifs – one using yarn C and one using yarn D.
Small motifs (make 2 in total)
Using yarn C, work as given for medium motif to end of round 2.
Fasten off.
Make a further one small motif using yarn D.
Using photograph as a guide, sew motifs in place.

54 [54: 54: 57: 57: 59] cm
(21½ [21½: 21½: 22½: 22½: 23] in)

42 [44: 46: 50: 52: 56] cm
(16½ [17½: 18: 19½: 20½: 22] in)

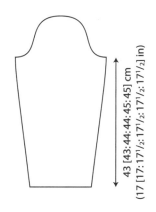

43 [43: 44: 44: 45: 45] cm
(17 [17: 17½: 17½: 17½: 17½] in)

Main image page 5

◼ ◼
AOIFE

by ANTONI & ALISON

SIZE

8	10	12	14	16	18	20	22

To fit bust

82	87	92	97	102	107	112	117	cm
32	34	36	38	40	42	44	46	in

YARN

Rowan Country

12	12	13	14	14	15	16	16	x 50gm

(photographed in Heather 655)

NEEDLES

1 pair 9mm (no 00) (US 13) needles
1 pair 10mm (no 000) (US 15) needles

BUTTONS – 2 x 00410

TENSION

10 sts and 14 rows to 10 cm measured over stocking stitch using 9mm (US 13) needles.

BACK

Using 9mm (US 13) needles cast on 43 [45: 47: 51: 53: 57: 59: 63] sts.
Work in g st for 4 rows, ending with RS facing for next row.
Beg with a K row, cont in st st until back meas 28 [28: 27: 30: 29: 31: 30: 32] cm, ending with RS facing for next row.
Shape raglan armholes
Cast off 3 sts at beg of next 2 rows.
37 [39: 41: 45: 47: 51: 53: 57] sts.
Dec 1 st at each end of next 1 [3: 3: 7: 7: 11: 11: 15] rows, then on every foll alt row to 19 [19: 19: 19: 21: 21: 21: 21] sts, then on foll row, ending with RS facing for next row.
Cast off rem 17 [17: 17: 17: 19: 19: 19: 19] sts.

LEFT FRONT

Using 9mm (US 13) needles cast on 21 [22: 23: 25: 26: 28: 29: 31] sts.
Work in g st for 4 rows, ending with RS facing for next row.
Beg with a K row, cont in st st until left front matches back to beg of raglan armhole shaping, ending with RS facing for next row.
Shape raglan armhole
Cast off 3 sts at beg of next row.
18 [19: 20: 22: 23: 25: 26: 28] sts.
Work 1 row.
Shape front slope
Dec 1 st at raglan armhole edge of next 1 [3: 3: 7: 7: 11: 11: 15] rows, then on foll 8 [7: 8: 6: 6: 4:

5: 3] alt rows and at same time dec 1 st at front slope edge of next and foll 4 [4: 3: 3: 5: 5: 4: 4] alt rows, then on 2 [2: 3: 3: 2: 2: 3: 3] foll 4th rows, ending with **WS** facing for next row. 2 sts.
Next row (WS): P2tog and fasten off.

RIGHT FRONT

Work to match left front, reversing shapings.

SLEEVES

Using 9mm (US 13) needles cast on 4 sts.
Work in g st for 8 rows, inc 1 st at each end of 2nd and every foll row. 18 sts.
Cast on 2 [2: 3: 3: 4: 4: 5: 5] sts at beg of next 2 rows.
22 [22: 24: 24: 26: 26: 28: 28] sts.
Place markers at both ends of last row.
Work in g st for a further 4 rows, ending with RS facing for next row.
Beg with a K row, cont in st st, shaping sides by inc 1 st at each end of 5th [5th: 5th: 5th: 9th: 9th: 9th: 9th] and every foll 12th [12th: 12th: 12th: 14th: 14th: 14th: 14th] row to 32 [32: 34: 34: 30: 30: 34: 34] sts, then on every foll – [–: –: –: 16th: 16th: 16th: 16th] row until there are – [–: –: –: 34: 34: 36: 36] sts.
Cont straight until sleeve meas 46 [46: 47: 47: 48: 48: 47: 47] cm **from markers**, ending with RS facing for next row.
Shape raglan
Cast off 3 sts at beg of next 2 rows.
26 [26: 28: 28: 28: 28: 30: 30] sts.
Dec 1 st at each end of next and foll 2 alt rows, then on 2 foll 4th rows, then on every foll alt row until 12 sts rem.
Work 1 row, ending with RS facing for next row.
Cast off rem 12 sts.

MAKING UP

Press as described on the information page.
Join raglan seams using back stitch, or mattress stitch if preferred.
Pockets (make 2)
Using 9mm (US 13) needles cast on 19 [21: 21: 23: 25: 27: 27: 29] sts.
Beg with a K row, work in st st for 12 cm, ending with RS facing for next row.
Work in g st, dec 0 [2: 2: 2: 2: 2: 2: 2] sts at each end of next 0 [1: 1: 2: 3: 4: 4: 5] rows, then 1 st at each end of foll 8 [7: 7: 6: 5: 4: 4: 3] rows, ending with RS facing for next row.
Cast off rem 3 sts.

Place pockets onto fronts, matching cast-on edge of pocket to top of g st section of front, and sew in place along side and lower edges. Fold g st section to RS and secure in place by attaching a button.

Left front band and collar

Using 10mm (US 15) needles cast on 5 sts.
Work in g st until band, when slightly stretched, fits up left front opening edge to beg of front slope shaping, ending with RS facing for next row.

Shape for collar

Cont in g st, inc 1 st at beg of next and every foll 4th row to 8 sts, then on every foll alt row until there are 18 [18: 19: 19: 19: 19: 20: 20] sts, ending with **WS** of band (RS of collar section) facing for next row.
Cast on 34 sts at beg of next row.
52 [52: 53: 53: 53: 53: 54: 54] sts.
Work 15 rows, ending with RS of collar (**WS** of band) facing for next row.
Cast off 14 sts at beg of next row.
38 [38: 39: 39: 39: 39: 40: 40] sts.
Work 1 row.
Cast on 14 sts at beg of next row.
Cont straight until collar, unstretched, fits up front slope and across to centre back neck, ending with **WS** of collar (RS of body) facing for next row.
Cast off.

Right front band and collar

Work to match left front band and collar, reversing shaping.

Slip st band and collar sections in place – cast-off edges of collar should meet at centre back neck but are NOT joined.

See information page for finishing instructions.

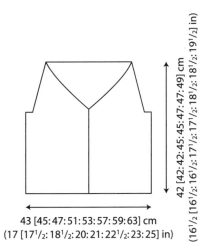

43 [45: 47: 51: 53: 57: 59: 63] cm
(17 [17½: 18½: 20: 21: 22½: 23: 25] in)

42 [42: 42: 45: 45: 47: 47: 49] cm
(16½ [16½: 16½: 17½: 17½: 18½: 18½: 19½] in)

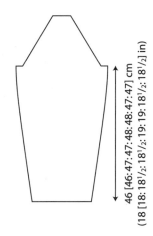

46 [46: 47: 47: 48: 48: 47: 47] cm
(18 [18: 18½: 18½: 19: 19: 18½: 18½] in)

Main image page 9 & 21

■ ■

DYLAN

by MARIE WALLIN

SIZE

	S	M	L	XL	XXL	
To fit chest						
	102	107	112	117	122	cm
	40	42	44	46	48	in

YARN

Rowan Country

| 17 | 18 | 19 | 21 | 22 | x 50gm |

(photographed in Birch 650)

NEEDLES

1 pair 8mm (no 0) (US 11) needles
1 pair 9mm (no 00) (US 13) needles
Cable needle

TENSION

10 sts and 14 rows to 10 cm measured over stocking stitch using 9mm (US 13) needles.

SPECIAL ABBREVIATIONS

Cr3R = slip next st onto cable needle and leave at back of work, K2, then P1 from cable needle;
Cr3L = slip next 2 sts onto cable needle and leave at front of work, P1, then K2 from cable needle;
C4B = slip next 2 sts onto cable needle and leave at back of work, K2, then K2 from cable needle;
C4F = slip next 2 sts onto cable needle and leave at front of work, K2, then K2 from cable needle;
Cr4R = slip next st onto cable needle and leave at back of work, K3, then P1 from cable needle;
Cr4L = slip next 3 sts onto cable needle and leave at front of work, P1, then K3 from cable needle;
C6B = slip next 3 sts onto cable needle and leave at back of work, K3, then K3 from cable needle;
C6F = slip next 3 sts onto cable needle and leave at front of work, K3, then K3 from cable needle.

BACK

Using 8mm (US 11) needles cast on 64 [66: 70: 72: 76] sts.
Row 1 (RS): *P1, K1, rep from * to end.
Row 2: As row 1.
Rows 3 and 4: *K1, P1, rep from * to end.
These 4 rows form double moss st.
Work in double moss st for 1 row more, ending with **WS** facing for next row.
Row 6 (WS): Patt 14 [15: 17: 18: 20] sts, M1, patt 11 sts, M1, patt 6 sts, M1, patt 2 sts, M1, patt 6 sts, M1, patt 11 sts, M1, patt to end.
70 [72: 76: 78: 82] sts.
Change to 9mm (US 13) needles.
Place chart
Row 1 (RS): Patt 4 sts, P5 [6: 8: 9: 11], work next 52 sts as row 1 of chart for body, P to last 4 sts, patt 4 sts.
Row 2: Patt 4 sts, K5 [6: 8: 9: 11], work next 52 sts as row 2 of chart for body, K to last 4 sts, patt 4 sts.
These 2 rows set the sts.
Noting that chart rows 1 and 2 are worked **once only** and then repeating chart rows 3 to 26 **throughout**, cont as set for a further 6 rows, ending with RS facing for next row.
Row 9 (RS): P9 [10: 12: 13: 15], work next 52 sts as row 9 of chart for body, P to end.
Row 10: K9 [10: 12: 13: 15], work next 52 sts as row 10 of chart for body, K to end.
These 2 rows set the sts for rest of back.
Cont as now set until back meas 39 [40: 39: 40: 39] cm, ending with RS facing for next row.
Shape armholes
Keeping patt correct, cast off 3 sts at beg of next 2 rows.

Body chart

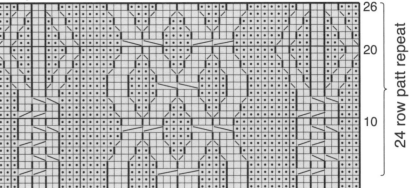

26
20
10
24 row patt repeat

64 [66: 70: 72: 76] sts.

Dec 1 st at each end of next 4 [3: 3: 2: 2] rows.

56 [60: 64: 68: 72] sts.

Cont straight until armhole meas 22 [23: 24: 25: 26] cm, ending with RS facing for next row.

Shape shoulders and back neck

Next row (RS): Cast off 5 [6: 6: 7: 8] sts, patt until there are 8 [9: 10: 11: 11] sts on right needle and turn, leaving rem sts on a holder.

Work each side of neck separately.

Cast off 3 sts at beg of next row.

Cast off rem 5 [6: 7: 8: 8] sts.

With RS facing, rejoin yarn to rem sts, cast off centre 30 [30: 32: 32: 34] sts dec 4 sts evenly, patt to end.

Complete to match first side, reversing shapings.

FRONT

Work as given for back until 8 [8: 10: 10: 12] rows less have been worked than on back to beg of shoulder shaping, ending with RS facing for next row.

Shape neck

Next row (RS): Patt 14 [16: 18: 20: 22] sts and turn, leaving rem sts on a holder.

Work each side of neck separately.

Dec 1 st at neck edge of next 3 rows, then on foll 1 [1: 1: 2: 2: 3] alt rows.

10 [12: 13: 15: 16] sts.

Work 2 rows, ending with RS facing for next row.

Shape shoulder

Cast off 5 [6: 6: 7: 8] sts at beg of next row.

Work 1 row.

Cast off rem 5 [6: 7: 8: 8] sts.

With RS facing, rejoin yarn to rem sts, cast off centre 28 sts, patt to end.

Complete to match first side, reversing shapings.

SLEEVES

Using 8mm (US 11) needles cast on 26 [28: 28: 30: 30] sts.

Work in double moss st as given for back for 5 rows, ending with **WS** facing for next row.

Row 6 (WS): Patt 6 [7: 7: 8: 8] sts, M1, patt 6 sts, M1, patt 2 sts, M1, patt 6 sts, M1, patt to end.

30 [32: 32: 34: 34] sts.

Change to 9mm (US 13) needles.

Place chart

Row 1 (RS): P5 [6: 6: 7: 7], work next 20 sts as row 1 of chart for sleeve, P to end.

Row 2: K5 [6: 6: 7: 7], work next 20 sts as row 2 of chart for sleeve, K to end.

These 2 rows set the sts.

Noting that chart rows 1 and 2 are worked **once only** and then repeating chart rows 3 to 26 **throughout**, cont as set, shaping sides by inc 1 st at each end of next and every foll 4th row to 48 [48: 50: 50: 52] sts, then on every foll 6th row until there are 56 [58: 60: 62: 64] sts, taking inc sts into rev st st.

Cont straight until sleeve meas 52 [54: 56: 58: 60] cm, ending with RS facing for next row.

Shape top

Keeping patt correct, cast off 3 sts at beg of next 2 rows. 50 [52: 54: 56: 58] sts.

Dec 1 st at each end of next 5 rows, then on every foll alt row to 38 sts, then on foll 9 rows, ending with RS facing for next row. 20 sts.

Cast off 4 sts at beg of next 2 rows.

Cast off rem 12 sts dec 2 sts evenly.

MAKING UP

Press as described on the information page.

Join right shoulder seam using back stitch, or mattress stitch if preferred.

Neckband

With RS facing and using 8mm (US 11) needles, pick up and knit 8 [8: 10: 10: 12] sts down left side of neck, 23 sts from front, 8 [8: 10: 10: 12] sts up right side of neck, then 26 [26: 28: 28: 30] sts from back. 65 [65: 71: 71: 77] sts.

Row 1 (WS): P1, *K1, P1, rep from * to end.

Rows 2 and 3: K1, *P1, K1, rep from * to end.

Row 4: As row 1.

These 4 rows form double moss st.

Work in double moss st until neckband meas 6 cm, ending with RS facing for next row.

Cast off in patt.

See information page for finishing instructions, setting in sleeves using the set-in method and leaving side seams open for first 14 rows.

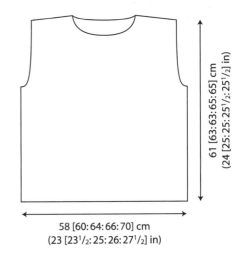

61 [63: 63: 65: 65] cm
(24 [25: 25: 25½: 25½] in)

58 [60: 64: 66: 70] cm
(23 [23½: 25: 26: 27½] in)

Sleeve chart

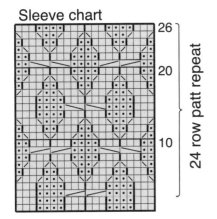

26

20

10

24 row patt repeat

Key

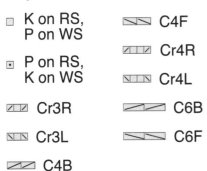

□ K on RS, P on WS

▫ P on RS, K on WS

Cr3R

Cr3L

C4B

C4F

Cr4R

Cr4L

C6B

C6F

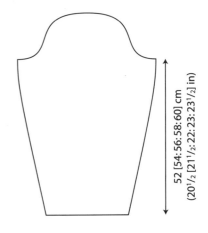

52 [54: 56: 58: 60] cm
(20½ [21½: 22: 23: 23½] in)

Main image page 15

ELVA SCARF

by MARIE WALLIN

YARN
Rowan Country

12   x 50gm

(photographed in Clover 656)

NEEDLES
1 pair 9mm (no 00) (US 13) needles
8.00mm (no 0) (US L11) crochet hook
Cable needle

TENSION
10 sts and 14 rows to 10 cm measured over stocking stitch using 9mm (US 13) needles.

SPECIAL ABBREVIATIONS
C2B = slip next st onto cable needle and leave at back of work, K1, then K1 from cable needle; **C2F** = slip next st onto cable needle and leave at front of work, K1, then K1 from cable needle; **Cr2R** = slip next st onto cable needle and leave at back of work, K1, then P1 from cable needle; **Cr2L** = slip next st onto cable needle and leave at front of work, P1, then K1 from cable needle; **Cr3R** = slip next st onto cable needle and leave at back of work, K2, then P1 from cable needle; **Cr3L** = slip next 2 sts onto cable needle and leave at front of work, P1, then K2 from cable needle; **Cr3RKPP** = slip next 2 sts onto cable needle and leave at back of work, K1, then P2 from cable needle; **Cr3LPPK** = slip next st onto cable needle and leave at front of work, P2, then K1 from cable needle; **C4B** = slip next 2 sts onto cable needle and leave at back of work, K2, then K2 from cable needle; **C4F** = slip next 2 sts onto cable needle and leave at front of work, K2, then K2 from cable needle; **Cr4R** = slip next 2 sts onto cable needle and leave at back of work, K2, then P2 from cable needle; **Cr4L** = slip next 2 sts onto cable needle and leave at front of work, P2, then K2 from cable needle; **MK** = (K1, P1, K1, P1, K1, P1, K1) all into next st, lift 2nd, 3rd, 4th, 5th, 6th and 7th sts on right needle over first st and off right needle.

UK CROCHET ABBREVIATIONS
ch = chain; **ss** = slip stitch; **dc** = double crochet.

US CROCHET ABBREVIATIONS
ch = chain; **ss** = slip stitch; **dc** = single crochet.

Key

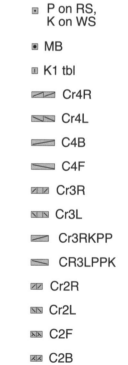

▨	K on RS, P on WS
▣	P on RS, K on WS
▦	MB
▥	K1 tbl
◿	Cr4R
◺	Cr4L
▱	C4B
▱	C4F
◿	Cr3R
◺	Cr3L
◿	Cr3RKPP
◺	CR3LPPK
◿	Cr2R
◺	Cr2L
◺	C2F
◿	C2B

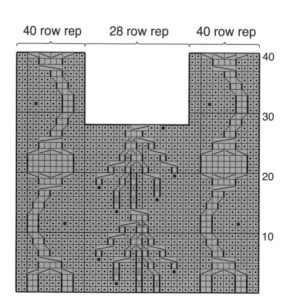

40 row rep   28 row rep   40 row rep

FINISHED SIZE
Completed scarf measures 30 cm (12 in) wide and 151 cm (59½ in) long, excluding pompon tassels.

SCARF
Using 9mm (US 13) needles cast on 42 sts.
Repeating the 40 or 28 row patt repeats throughout and noting that chart row 1 is a **WS** row, cont in patt from chart until scarf meas 150 cm, ending with RS facing for next row.

Cast off but do NOT fasten off.

MAKING UP
Press as described on the information page.
Crochet edging
With RS facing and using 8.00mm (US L11) crochet hook, slip loop from end of cast-off edge onto hook, 1 ch (does NOT count as st), work 1 round of dc evenly around entire outer edge of scarf, ending with ss to first dc.

Fasten off.
Pompon tassels (make 8)
Using 8.00mm (US L11) crochet hook, make 20 ch and fasten off.
Make two 6 cm diameter pompons. Attach one pompon to end of ch, and other pompon at random along rem length of ch.
Make a further 7 pompon tassels in this way.
Using photograph as a guide, attach 4 pompon tassels along each short end of scarf.

Main image page 7

NIAMH
by MARIE WALLIN

SIZE

	S	M	L	
To fit bust				
	82-87	92-97	102-107	cm
	32-34	36-38	40-42	in

YARN
Rowan Country

	11	12	13	x 50gm

(photographed in Rose 657)

NEEDLES
1 pair 8mm (no 0) (US 11) needles
1 pair 9mm (no 00) (US 13) needles
8.00mm (no 0) (US L11) crochet hook

TENSION
10 sts and 14 rows to 10 cm measured over stocking stitch using 9mm (US 13) needles.

UK CROCHET ABBREVIATIONS
ch = chain; **dc** = double crochet.

US CROCHET ABBREVIATIONS
ch = chain; **dc** = single crochet.

BACK
Using 9mm (US 13) needles cast on 62 [68: 74] sts.
Beg with a K row, work in st st until back meas 54 [56: 58] cm, ending with RS facing for next row.

Shape shoulders and back neck
Cast off, placing markers either side of centre 22 [22: 24] sts to denote back neck.

LEFT FRONT
Using 9mm (US 13) needles cast on 11 [14: 15] sts.
Beg with a K row, work in st st as folls:
Work 1 row, ending with **WS** facing for next row.
Row 2 (WS): P1, M1, P to end.
Row 3: K to last st, M1, K1.
Working all increases as set by last 2 rows, inc 1 st at shaped edge of next 26 [26: 28] rows, then on foll 2 alt rows.
41 [44: 47] sts.
Work 1 row, ending with RS facing for next row.
Shape front slope
Next row (RS): K to last 3 sts, K2tog, K1.
Next row: P1, P2tog, P to end.
Working all decreases as set by last 2 rows, dec 1 st at front slope edge of next 9 [7: 7] rows, then on foll 7 [9: 10] alt rows, then on every foll 4th row until 20 [23: 25] sts rem.
Cont straight until left front matches back to shoulder cast-off, ending with RS facing for next row.
Shape shoulder
Cast off.

RIGHT FRONT
Using 9mm (US 13) needles cast on 11 [14: 15] sts.
Beg with a K row, work in st st as folls:
Work 1 row, ending with **WS** facing for next row.
Row 2 (WS): P to last st, M1, P1.
Row 3: K1, M1, K to end.
Working all increases as set by last 2 rows, inc 1 st at shaped edge of next 26 [26: 28] rows, then on foll 2 alt rows.

41 [44: 47] sts.

Work 1 row, ending with RS facing for next row.

Shape front slope

Next row (RS): K1, sl 1, K1, psso, K to end.

Next row: P to last 3 sts, P2tog tbl, P1.

Working all decreases as set by last 2 rows, dec 1 st at front slope edge of next 9 [7: 7] rows, then on foll 7 [9: 10] alt rows, then on every foll 4th row until 20 [23: 25] sts rem.

Cont straight until right front matches back to shoulder cast-off, ending with RS facing for next row.

Shape shoulder

Cast off.

MAKING UP

Press as described on the information page.

Join both shoulder seams using back stitch, or mattress stitch if preferred.

Armhole borders (both alike)

Mark points along side seam edges 20 [21: 22] cm either side of shoulder seams.

With RS facing and using 8mm (US 11) needles, pick up and knit 47 [49: 51] sts along armhole edge between markers.

Change to 9mm (US 13) needles.

Row 1 (WS): P1, *K1, P1, rep from * to end.

Row 2: K1, *P1, K1, rep from * to end.

These 2 rows form rib.

Cont in rib until armhole border meas 5 cm, ending with RS facing for next row.

Cast off in rib.

Join side and armhole border seams, leaving a small opening in right side seam level with beg of front slope shaping.

Neck and lower edging

With RS facing and using 8.00mm (US L11) crochet hook, attach yarn to edge st at beg of right front slope, 1 ch (does NOT count as st), 1 dc into place where yarn was joined, *miss 2 row-ends, 5 dc into next row-end, rep from * to end, replacing 5 dc at end of last rep with 1 dc into edge st at beg of left front slope.

Work lower edging

Now make a length of ch 100 cm long but do NOT fasten off.

Using photograph as a guide, sew this length of chain to lower front opening and hem edge to form a wave effect, making more ch as required, until opposite end of neck edging is reached. Cont in this way, making and attaching a second line of waves to complete edging as in photograph, ending at end of neck edging row. Fasten off.

Work wave edging around cast-off edges of armhole borders in same way, beg and ending at underarm seam.

Ties (make 2)

Using 8.00mm (US L11) crochet hook, make a ch approx 110 [120: 130] cm long.

Row 1: 1 dc into 2nd ch from hook, 1 dc into each ch to end.

Fasten off.

Attach a tie to each front opening edge, level with beg of front slope shaping.

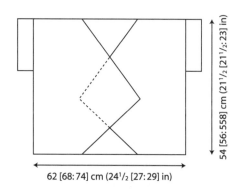

54 [56: 558] cm (21½ [21½: 23] in)

62 [68: 74] cm (24½ [27: 29] in)

AUSTRALIA:
Australian Country Spinners,
314 Albert Street, Brunswick,
Victoria 3056
Tel: (61) 3 9380 3888 Fax: (61) 3 9387 2674
E-mail: sales@auspinners.com.au

BELGIUM:
Pavan,
Meerlaanstraat 73, B9860 Balegem (Oosterzele).
Tel: (32) 9 221 8594   Fax: (32) 9 221 8594
E-mail: pavan@pandora.be

CANADA:
Diamond Yarn,
9697 St Laurent, Montreal, Quebec, H3L 2N1
Tel: (514) 388 6188

Diamond Yarn (Toronto),
155 Martin Ross, Unit 3, Toronto, Ontario, M3J 2L9
Tel: (416) 736 6111   Fax: (416) 736 6112
E-mail: diamond@diamondyarn.com
www.diamondyarn.com

DENMARK:
Coats Danmark A/S, Mariendlunds Alle 4, 7430 Ikast
Tel: (45) 96 60 34 00   Fax: (45) 96 60 34 08
Email: coats@coats.dk

FINLAND:
Coats Opti Oy,
Ketjutie 3, 04220 Kerava
Tel: (358) 9 274 871 Fax: (358) 9 2748 7330
E-mail: coatsopti.sales@coats.com

FRANCE:
Coats France / Steiner Frères,
100, avenue du Général de Gaulle,
18 500 Mehun-Sur-Yèvre
Tel: (33) 02 48 23 12 30   Fax: (33) 02 48 23 12 40

GERMANY:
Coats GMbH,
Kaiserstrasse 1, D-79341 Kenzingen
Tel: (49) 7644 8020   Fax: (49) 7644 802399.
www.coatsgmbh.de

HOLLAND:
de Afstap,
Oude Leliestraat 12, 1015 AW Amsterdam
Tel: (31) 20 6231445 Fax: (31) 20 427 8522

HONG KONG:
East Unity Co Ltd,
Unit B2, 7/F Block B, Kailey Industrial Centre,
12 Fung Yip Street, Chai Wan
Tel: (852) 2869 7110 Fax: (852) 2537 6952
E-mail: eastuni@netvigator.com

ICELAND:
Storkurinn, Laugavegi 59, 101 Reykjavik
Tel: (354) 551 8258
Fax: (354) 562 8252
E-mail: malin@mmedia.is

ITALY: D.L.
srl, Via Piave,
24 – 26, 20016 Pero, Milan
Tel: (39) 02 339 10 180 Fax: (39) 02 33914661

JAPAN:
Puppy Co Ltd,
T151-0051, 3-16-5 Sendagaya, Shibuyaku, Tokyo
Tel: (81) 3 3490 2827 Fax: (81) 3 5412 7738
E-mail: info@rowan-jaeger.com

KOREA:
Coats Korea Co Ltd,
5F Kuckdong B/D, 935-40 Bangbae- Dong,
Seocho-Gu, Seoul
Tel: (82) 2 521 6262. Fax: (82) 2 521 5181

NEW ZEALAND:
Please contact Rowan for details of stockists

NORWAY:
Coats Knappehuset AS,
Pb 100 Ulste, 5873 Bergen
Tel: (47) 55 53 93 00   Fax: (47) 55 53 93 93

SINGAPORE:
Golden Dragon Store,
101 Upper Cross Street #02-51, People's Park
Centre, Singapore 058357
Tel: (65) 6 5358454 Fax : (65) 6 2216278
E-mail: gdscraft@hotmail.com

SOUTH AFRICA:
Arthur Bales PTY,
PO Box 44644, Linden 2104
Tel: (27) 11 888 2401 Fax: (27) 11 782 6137

SPAIN:
Oyambre,
Pau Claris 145, 80009 Barcelona.
Tel: (34) 670 011957   Fax: (34) 93 4872672
E-mail: oyambre@oyambreonline.com

SWEDEN:
Coats Expotex AB,
Division Craft, Box 297, 401 24 Grteborg
Tel: (46) 33 720 79 00 Fax: 46 31 47 16 50

TAIWAN:
Laiter Wool Knitting Co Ltd,
10-1 313 Lane, Sec 3, Chung Ching North Road,
Taipei
Tel: (886) 2 2596 0269 Fax : (886) 2 2598 0619

Mon Cher Corporation,
9F No 117 Chung Sun First Road, Kaoshiung
Tel: (886) 7 9711988   Fax: (886) 7 9711666

U.S.A.:
Westminster Fibers Inc,
4 Townsend West, Suite 8, Nashua,
New Hampshire 03063
Tel: (1 603) 886 5041 / 5043 Fax (1 603) 886 1056
E-mail: rowan@westminsterfibers.com

U.K:
Rowan,
Green Lane Mill, Holmfirth, West Yorkshire,
England HD9 2DX
Tel: +44 (0) 1484 681881 Fax: +44 (0) 1484 687920
E-mail: mail@knitrowan.com
Inernet: www.knitrowan.com

For stockists in all other countries please contact
Rowan for stockist details.

CROCHET STITCHES

Although the crochet effects used within these designs may seem daunting to the beginner, they are actually very simple and use the very basic crochet stitches.

We hope this article will explain the basic stitches needed to complete the designs within Country Escape, and encourage everyone to pick up a crochet hook and 'have a go'. You will be surprised how easy it is and once you have mastered the basics, you can then go onto create some beautiful effects.

MAKING A CHAIN STITCH (CH) AND FOUNDATION CHAIN.

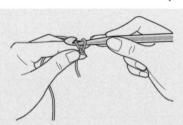 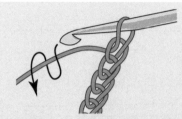 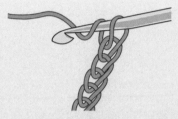

1. All crochet is started by making a slip knot in exactly the same way as you would begin knitting. Slip this knot onto the crochet hook and you're ready to make your first foundation chain. As when knitting, this slip knot is your first stitch.

2. Hold the crochet hook in your right hand

and grip the base of the slip knot between the thumb and first finger of the left hand. Wind the ball end of the yarn (working) around the fingers of your left hand to control the tension – exactly as you would when knitting but on the other hand. To make the first **chain**, twist the hook back and under the working strand of yarn so

that it loops around the hook. Pull this new loop of yarn through the loop already on the hook and you have made another chain.

3. Continue in this way, drawing new loops of yarn through the loop on the hook, until you have made the required number of chains.

MAKING A SLIP STITCH (SS).

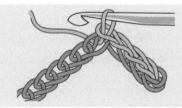

1. A **slip stitch** is the very shortest and easiest of the basic stitches. To work a slip stitch, insert the hook into the work and take the yarn over the hook in the same

way as if you were going to make a chain stitch. Pull this new loop of yarn through both the work and the loop on the hook – this completes the slip stitch.

MAKING A DOUBLE CROCHET (DC) AMERICAN SINGLE CROCHET (SC)

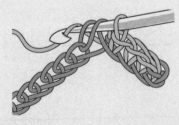  

1. The next tallest stitch, the **double crochet** is one of the two most commonly used crochet stitches. This is worked in a similar way to a slip stitch. Start by inserting the hook into the work, and taking the yarn over the hook.

2. Draw this new loop through just the work, leaving two loops on the hook.

3. Take the yarn over the hook again. Draw this new loop through both the loops on the hook thereby completing the double crochet stitch.

MAKING A TREBLE (TR) AMERICAN DOUBLE CROCHET (DC)

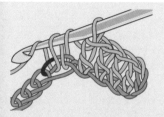 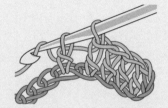  

1. The other most commonly used crochet stitch is the **treble**. To make a treble start by taking the yarn over the hook BEFORE inserting into the work.

2. Then insert the hook into the work, take

the yarn over the hook again and draw this new loop through. There are now three loops on the hook.

3. Take the yarn over the hook and draw this new loop through the first two loops only

on the hook. There are now two loops on the hook.

4. Take the yarn over the hook, and draw this through the remaining two loops on the hook to complete the treble stitch.

MAKING A DOUBLE TREBLE (DTR) AMERICAN TREBLE (TR)

1. The taller **double treble** is worked as for the treble, except that the yarn is wrapped around the hook twice before it is inserted into the work. To begin take the yarn twice round the hook. Insert the hook into the work, take the yarn over the hook and draw through the work. There are now four loops on the hook. Take the yarn over the

hook and draw through the first two loops only on the hook. There are now three loops on the hook. Continue taking the yarn over the hook and drawing through two loops at a time until just one loop remains. The double treble is now complete.

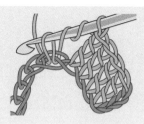

WORKING IN ROUNDS.

1. To start a piece of circular crochet, begin by making the foundation chain. Now secure the ends of this chain to each other by working a slip stitch into the first chain to form a loop.

2. Make sure you don't twist the chain before you join the ends as this could make the work

twisted or the stitches uneven. The first 'round' of crochet is worked into the ring. The instructions in the pattern will tell you which stitches and how many need to be worked.

3. At the end of each round you will need to secure the last stitch to the first stitch to close

the round. Do this by working a slip stitch into the top of the first stitch. Also in following rounds the stitches need to be raised, this is done by working twice into the same stitch were instructed. The work is not turned at the end of a round, so the right side is always facing you.

FASTENING OFF.

To fasten off your crochet work, cut the yarn about 8cm from the work. Pass this loose end through the one remaining loop

on the hook and pull tight. Darn the loose ends into the back of the work, using a blunt ended needle.

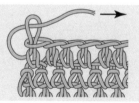

INFORMATION

TENSION

Obtaining the correct tension is perhaps the single factor which can make the difference between a successful garment and a disastrous one. It controls both the shape and size of an article, so any variation, however slight, can distort the finished garment. Different designers feature in our books and it is **their** tension, given at the **start** of each pattern, which you must match. We recommend that you knit a square in pattern and/or stocking stitch (depending on the pattern instructions) of perhaps 5 - 10 more stitches and 5 - 10 more rows than those given in the tension note. Mark out the central 10cm square with pins. If you have too many stitches to 10cm try again using thicker needles, if you have too few stitches to 10cm try again using finer needles. Once you have achieved the correct tension your garment will be knitted to the measurements indicated in the size diagram shown at the end of the pattern.

SIZING & SIZE DIAGRAM NOTE

The instructions are given for the smallest size. Where they vary, work the figures in brackets for the larger sizes. **One set of figures refers to all sizes.** Included with most patterns in this brochure is a 'size diagram', or sketch of the finished garment and its dimensions. The size diagram shows the finished width of the garment at the under-arm point, and it is this measurement that the knitter should choose first; a useful tip is to measure one of your own garments which is a comfortable fit. Having chosen a size based on width, look at the corresponding length for that size; if you are not happy with the total length which we recommend, adjust your own garment before beginning your armhole shaping - any adjustment after this point will mean that your sleeve will not fit into your garment easily - don't forget to take your adjustment into account if there is any side seam shaping. Finally, look at the sleeve length; the size diagram shows the finished sleeve measurement, taking into account any top-arm insertion length. Measure your body between the centre of your neck and your wrist, this measurement should correspond to half the garment width plus the sleeve length. Again, your sleeve length may be adjusted, but remember to take into consideration your sleeve increases if you do adjust the length - you must increase more frequently than the pattern states to shorten your sleeve, less frequently to lengthen it.

CHART NOTE

Many of the patterns in the brochure are worked from charts. Each square on a chart represents a stitch and each line of squares a row of knitting. Each colour used is given a different letter and these are shown in the **materials** section, or in the **key** alongside the chart of each pattern. When working from the charts, read odd rows (K) from right to left and even rows (P) from left to right, unless otherwise stated.

KNITTING WITH COLOUR

There are two main methods of working colour into a knitted fabric: **Intarsia** and **Fairisle** techniques. The first method produces a single thickness of fabric and is usually used where a colour is only required in a particular area of a row and does not form a repeating pattern across the row, as in the fairisle technique.
Intarsia: The simplest way to do this is to cut short lengths of yarn for each motif or block of colour used in a row. Then joining in the various colours at the appropriate point on the row, link one colour to the next by twisting them around each other where they meet on the wrong side to avoid gaps. All ends can then either be darned along the colour join lines, as each motif is completed or then can be " knitted-in" to the fabric of the knitting as each colour is worked into the pattern. This is done in much the same way as "weaving- in" yarns when working the Fairisle technique and does save time darning-in ends. It is essential that the tension is noted for **Intarsia** as this may vary from the stocking stitch if both are used in the same pattern.
Fairisle type knitting: When two or three colours are worked repeatedly across a row, strand the yarn **not** in use loosely behind the stitches being worked. If you are working with more than two colours, treat the "floating" yarns as if they were one yarn and always spread the stitches to their correct width to keep them elastic. It is advisable not to carry the stranded or "floating" yarns over more than three stitches at a time, but to weave them under and over the colour you are working. The "floating" yarns are therefore caught at the back of the work.

FINISHING INSTRUCTIONS

After working for hours knitting a garment, it seems a great pity that many garments are spoiled because such little care is taken in the pressing and finishing process. Follow the following tips for a truly professional-looking garment.

PRESSING

Block out each piece of knitting and following the instructions on the ball band press the garment pieces, omitting the ribs. Tip: Take special care to press the edges, as this will make sewing up both easier and neater. If the ball band indicates that the fabric is not to be pressed, then covering the blocked out fabric with a damp white cotton cloth and leaving it to stand will have the desired effect. Darn in all ends neatly along the selvage edge or a colour join, as appropriate.

STITCHING

When stitching the pieces together, remember to match areas of colour and texture very carefully where they meet. Use a seam stitch such as back stitch or mattress stitch for all main knitting seams and join all ribs and neckband with mattress stitch, unless otherwise stated.

CONSTRUCTION

Having completed the pattern instructions, join left shoulder and neckband seams as detailed above. Sew the top of the sleeve to the body of the garment using the method detailed in the pattern, referring to the appropriate guide:
Shallow set-in sleeves: Match decreases at beg of armhole shaping to decreases at top of sleeve. Sew sleeve head into armhole, easing in shapings.
Set- in sleeves: Place centre of cast-off edge of sleeve to shoulder seam. Set in sleeve, easing sleeve head into armhole.

Join side and sleeve seams.
Slip stitch pocket edgings and linings into place.
Sew on buttons to correspond with buttonholes.
Ribbed welts and neckbands and any areas of garter stitch should not be pressed.

Cross stitch

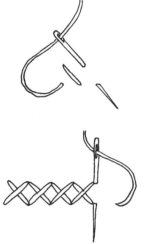

Running stitch